Adam Smith

Titles in the series *Critical Lives* present the work of leading cultural figures of the modern period. Each book explores the life of the artist, writer, philosopher or architect in question and relates it to their major works.

In the same series

Adam Smith

Jonathan Conlin

REAKTION BOOKS

Published by Reaktion Books Ltd
Unit 32, Waterside
44–48 Wharf Road
London N1 7UX, UK
www.reaktionbooks.co.uk

First published 2016

Printed and bound in Great Britain by Bell & Bain, Glasgow

A catalogue record for this book is available from the British Library

ISBN 978 1 78023 568 4

Contents

Note on the Text

All quotations, with original spellings, are taken from *The Glasgow Edition of the Works and Correspondence of Adam Smith*, edited by R. H. Campbell and A. S. Skinner, published between 1975 and 1987 by Oxford University Press, and also available in inexpensive paperback form from Liberty Fund Press.

C	*Correspondence of Adam Smith*, ed. E. C. Mossner and I. S. Ross
EPS	*Essays on Philosophical Subjects*, ed. W.P.D. Wightman, J. C. Bryce and I. S. Ross
LJ	*Lectures on Jurisprudence*, ed. R. L. Meek, D. D. Raphael and P. G. Stein
LRBL	*Lectures on Rhetoric and Belles Lettres*, ed. J. C. Bryce
TMS	*The Theory of Moral Sentiments*, ed. A. L. Macfie and D. D. Raphael
WN	*An Inquiry into the Nature and Causes of the Wealth of Nations*, ed. William B. Todd

Introduction

The eighteenth-century Scottish thinker Adam Smith (1723–1790)
is considered to be the founding father of free market economics.
Unlike many twentieth- and twenty-first-century practitioners
of economics, however, Adam Smith preferred telling stories to
writing equations; homespun tales about routine interactions
and everyday objects, about 'things of a very frivolous nature' that
nonetheless revealed something important about the nature of man
(*TMS*, 17). Smith's surviving works originated as lectures written for
delivery to undergraduates at the University of Glasgow. Although
the Scottish education system was one of the finest around in the
eighteenth-century world, were we able to travel back and sit in on
one of Professor Smith's classes we would immediately be struck by
how young the audience was. Smith was lecturing teenagers aged
between fourteen to sixteen (between 7:30 am and 8:30 am, no less),
which explains some, but not all, of his fondness for telling stories.

Smith's eighteenth-century prose can make reading his work
something of a challenge. He may have been lecturing to teenagers,
but it can feel as if Smith is speaking a dead language. This book
will suggest that this problem lies as much in our failure to listen
correctly as to any shift in vocabulary or any weaknesses in
Smith's thought. Until fairly recently the only people listening to
Smith were economists, and some philosophers. Even then, each
expected Smith to 'speak their language' and became inattentive,
frustrated or bored when Smith failed to do so. As with many great

William Hogarth, *Scholars at a Lecture*, 1736, etching and engraving. Adam Smith's students presumably paid more attention than the students depicted here.

thinkers of the past, were he to return to life Smith would probably be surprised by what his self-proclaimed followers have done in his name. He would be frustrated by the tendency to draw a line between his study of 'political economy', that is, of the best means of promoting 'opulence' in a nation, and his 'moral philosophy', his attempt to advance a set of moral principles grounded in human nature. One of the teenagers sitting in Professor Smith's class in

1766 transcribed the following pithy summary, which presents
these investigations as equally necessary and interlocking:

> In order to consider the means proper to produce opulence it
> will be proper to consider what opulence and plenty consist in,
> or what are those things which ought to abound in a nation.
> To this it will also be previously necessary to consider what
> are the naturall wants and demands of mankind. Man has
> received from the bounty of nature reason and ingenuity, art,
> contrivan[c]e, and capacity of improvement far superior to what
> she has bestowed on any of the other animalls, but is at the
> same time in a much more helpless and [dependent] condition
> with regard to the support and comfort of his life (*LJ*, 333).

In the nineteenth century economists subjected Smith to a
swingeing edit, focusing exclusively on his *An Inquiry into the
Nature and Causes of the Wealth of Nations* (1776). In the Glasgow
Edition (the definitive edition, from which all quotations are taken)
The Wealth of Nations is 947 pages long. Apart from a chapter on
export rebates and a long digression on the origins of the national
debt, it is an accessible text that well repays reading. It is certainly
much more enjoyable than other landmarks in the history of
economic thought, such as John Maynard Keynes's *General Theory
of Employment, Interest and Money* (1936). Economists cut *The
Wealth of Nations* down to three pages. Three stories. These came
to define 'Adam Smith', and if today's undergraduate economists
or MBA students study Smith at all, this is all the Smith they get.

The first story tells of how productivity increases as a result of the
specialization of labour. Smith focuses on the manufacturing of pins:

> To take an example, therefore, from a very trifling manufacture;
> but one in which the division of labour has been very often taken
> notice of, the trade of the pin-maker; a workman not educated

to this business (which the division of labour has rendered a distinct trade), nor acquainted with the use of the machinery employed in it (to the invention of which the same division of labour has probably given occasion), could scarce, perhaps, with his utmost industry, make one pin in a day, and certainly could not make twenty. But in the way in which this business is now carried on, not only the whole work is a peculiar [i.e. distinct] trade, but it is divided into a number of branches, of which the greater part are likewise peculiar trades. One man draws out the wire, another straights it, a third cuts it, a fourth points it, a fifth grinds it at the top for receiving the head; to make the head requires two or three distinct operations; to put it on, is a peculiar business, to whiten the pins is another; it is even a trade by itself to put them into the paper; and the important business of making a pin is, in this manner, divided into about eighteen distinct operations. [A workshop of ten men could] though they were very poor, and therefore but indifferently accommodated with the necessary machinery . . . when they exerted themselves, make among them about twelve pounds of pins in a day. There are in a pound upwards of four thousand pins of a middling size. Those ten persons, therefore, could make among them upwards of forty-eight thousand pins in a day (*WN*, 14–15).

Smith's pin factory is an important story that makes several salient points, some of which will be explored in later chapters. First, it should remind us that the benefits of breaking down manufacturing operations into many small steps were recognized long before the existence of the assembly line. Smith is writing a century and a half before Henry Ford's Detroit factory started pumping out Model T cars, yet he does not see the division of labour as anything new. On the contrary, it 'has been very often taken notice of'; indeed, it had been noted by the English philosopher Sir William Petty in the seventeenth century. Smith also notes how the division of labour has made mechanization possible. In this and other passages he describes how the workmen themselves innovate, coming up with short cuts or other devices that increase productivity.

Smith divides human history into four stages, beginning with the 'Age of Hunters'. In this stage every individual has to play a number of parts: child-minder, hunter, gatherer, spear-maker, potter, cook, tailor and so on. Jack of all trades, he is master of none, and productivity is poor. So is quality: the clothes are draughty, the pots wobbly and the meat (assuming the spears work) isn't that nice either. Nobody has much opportunity to refine their skills through practice, because they are only supplying their own needs. Even if they had the time and materials to focus on making pots, there would be little point, because a single person needs only so many pots.

But if each caveman can exchange his surplus, then everything changes. The spear-maker finds his needs for pots, meat and other necessities are better and more quickly served by making extra spears and exchanging them with the caveman potter and the caveman hunter, rather than trying to fashion his own pots and do his own hunting. Everyone benefits. With better weapons, practised hunters and improved storage, the food supply becomes more reliable and secure. Society itself becomes more interdependent, and therefore stronger. It would take a foolish tribe to pick a fight with Smith's cavemen: not only are they better fed and armed, but they are used to cooperating. They can also communicate better. For even without money the cavemen haggle over the exchange of their products, and so language develops (*TMS*, 336). 'Nobody ever saw a dog make a fair and deliberate exchange of one bone for another with another dog', Smith notes (*WN*, 26). Nor has anyone ever seen dogs use language. For Smith these two observations are related.

This leads us to the second of the three familiar stories. Like the pin factory story, this one comes very early on in *The Wealth of Nations*:

Humans have been making pins for a long time. This bronze-cast pin from western Iran dates from the 2nd millennium BCE.

> It is not from the benevolence of the butcher, the brewer, or
> the baker, that we expect our dinner, but from their regard
> to their own interest. We address ourselves, not to their
> humanity but to their self-love, and never talk to them of
> our own necessities but of their advantages (*WN*, 26–7).

This passage has typically been read as an argument in favour
of viewing individuals in the marketplace as motivated solely
by self-interest, narrowly defined. Markets work, it is suggested,
only if everyone in them is fixated solely on the greedy pursuit of
their own advantage. Humanity (what Smith normally refers to
as 'benevolence') and other noble sentiments are out of place in
markets, and are rightly kept out. The market is a different country.
We behave differently there. It may demand that we temporarily
suspend those nobler sentiments that we express in other spheres
of action. But hey, that's the price of doing business. It's nothing
personal.

All of us derive benefit from what goes on 'in there', so we
should be wary of looking too closely or moralizing, for fear of
becoming hypocrites. Gung-ho advocates of amoral capitalism
go further and see the market as a source of normative behaviour,
the place where 'real life' is to be found, where fine talk of virtue
and justice is silenced and we confront our true selves, warts and
all. Gordon Gekko's famous speech in the Oliver Stone film *Wall
Street* (1987) may be taken as an example of this. Here is Gekko
appealing to fellow shareholders of a fictional paper company,
inviting them to support his hostile takeover of the firm:

> The point is, ladies and gentlemen, that greed, for lack of a better
> word, is good. Greed is right. Greed works. Greed clarifies, cuts
> through and captures the essence of the evolutionary spirit.
> Greed, in all of its forms – greed for life, for money, for love,
> knowledge – has marked the upward surge of mankind and

'Greed is good': Michael Douglas as Gordon Gekko in Oliver Stone's *Wall Street*.

greed, you mark my words, will not only save Teldar Paper, but that other malfunctioning corporation called the USA.

Smith does not applaud this greedy, 'dog eat dog' variety of capitalism (nor, as we have seen, does he think dogs know a thing about markets). This is not because he wants to escape the market, or because he fails to recognize what Gekko calls the 'evolutionary spirit'. On the contrary, it was reading *The Wealth of Nations* that helped Charles Darwin come up with the theory of evolution by natural selection in the 1830s.[1] According to Smith, 'a certain propensity in human nature . . . to truck, barter and exchange one thing for another' – what might be called the trading instinct – lies at the heart of what makes us human (*WN*, 25). Were he alive today Smith would find the idea of 'the market' as a separate sphere deeply strange. The assumption that everyone in the market is a 'rational utility maximizer' was famously proposed by Gary Becker in his *Economic Approaches to Human Behaviour* (1976). As we shall see, Smith is highly sceptical of our ability to discern where our own interests lie. As for 'reason' and 'utility', these are fine machines for philosophers to tinker with, but far too remote to motivate the actions of you or I.

The next story isn't really a story, but rather a character – or rather a limb, and an insubstantial one at that: the invisible hand. *The Wealth of Nations* may be almost a thousand pages long, but the invisible hand appears (if an invisible hand can be said to appear) only once, on page 456. Smith explains that every person who has money to invest 'necessarily' tries to invest it where it will produce the greatest profit. He will prefer to invest it at home rather than abroad because it is easier to keep an eye on:

> As every individual, therefore, endeavours as much as he can both to employ his capital in the support of domestick industry, and so to direct that industry that its produce may be of the greatest value; every individual necessarily labours to render the annual revenue of the society as great as he can. He generally, indeed, neither intends to promote the publick interest, nor knows how much he is promoting it. By preferring the support of domestick to that of foreign industry, he intends only his own security; and by directing that industry in such a manner as its produce may be of the greatest value, he intends only his own gain, and he is in this, as in many other cases, led by an invisible hand to promote an end which was no part of his intention. Nor is it always the worse for the society that it was no part of it. By pursuing his own interest he frequently promotes that of the society more effectually than when he really intends to promote it. I have never known much good done by those who affected to trade for the publick good. It is an affectation, indeed, not very common among merchants, and very few words need be employed in dissuading them from it (*WN*, 456).

Smith writes that there are 'many other cases' where this kind of law of unintended consequences can be seen in action. It is striking, therefore, that he should have only mentioned the invisible hand once in *The Wealth of Nations,* once in his earlier work *The Theory of Moral Sentiments* (1759) and once in an intriguing essay on the history of astronomy.

Smith formed part of that broader movement we call the Enlightenment. In his essay 'What is Enlightenment?', of 1784, the German philosopher Immanuel Kant defines enlightenment as 'man's emergence from self-imposed immaturity'. He in turn defines 'immaturity' as the inability to use one's understanding without someone else's guidance. That this immaturity is self-imposed is striking, in so far as the history of the eighteenth-century European Enlightenment is often told as an institutional or political project involving churches, states, a rising bourgeoisie, a free press and abstract notions of public opinion. Then, as now, it can often

Can we love an invisible hand? Attributed to Marco Benefial, *Youth Kissing an Outstretched Hand, c.* 1720, red chalk.

seem as if immaturity is imposed by others, rather than a matter of personal choice. Yet Kant briefly runs through a number of ways in which immaturity can be a choice, and can reasonably appear the easy option. To outsource thought to other people saves time, effort and anxiety. Despite this rather gloomy analysis of human nature Kant is nonetheless optimistic for mankind's long-term future: with freedom, he concludes, 'public enlightenment' is 'almost inevitable'.[2] Smith is not so optimistic. Like us, perhaps, he would be surprised to find one of his most sensitive readers writing (in 1999) of how 'the march of the liberal Enlightenment seems irresistible'.[3]

Kant does not just see us as running the risk of outsourcing thought to individuals such as rulers or priests. He is equally concerned about the risks of outsourcing thought to 'rules and formulas'. Though disembodied and impersonal, these are just as capable of taking the strain off our own minds. 'Rules and formulas, those mechanical aids to the rational use, or rather misuse, of his natural gifts, are the shackles of a permanent immaturity', Kant writes. Self-proclaimed advocates of Adam Smith have made the invisible hand into such a shackle. In lobbying government, business interests have repeatedly cautioned the state against this or that measure on the grounds that it might interfere with the invisible hand. This fetishization has not limited itself to questions of state regulation. Although Smith is careful to note that his invisible hand worked its magic within a 'well-governed state', all too often the invisible hand has been proposed as a replacement for state government – indeed, for any government at all.

Smith sees the main threat to the invisible hand as being these same 'men of business', not the state. This is not surprising, as businessmen had been busy restricting trade centuries before the emergence of states and statesmanship. Established in medieval Europe to regulate a specific trade, guilds were a powerful regulatory force, albeit one that was in decline by Smith's day. Each guild had its own hall, symbols, rituals and internal hierarchy. In many cases guilds controlled a city's government. The guilds' main purpose was to protect the 'mystery' of their trade or profession from outside competition. Though they struggled to achieve full guild status, the pin-makers of medieval London otherwise afford a suitably Smithian example. The Pinners' first set of regulations for their industry dates back to 1356. According to these, no non-member could 'hold house or shop' in London or its suburbs 'nor sell nor buy anything concerned with the craft' without being examined by the 'masters of the craft' and paying a fee. Only a 'master' could take on apprentices; nobody could work on the weekend or during certain weekday hours. A woman could not make pins at any time, unless she was the wife or daughter of a paid-up 'master'. The 'umper' of the craft would inspect all workshops and all wares, fining masters who produced substandard pins or 'hawked' their wares (by selling at fairs, for example) – the pins in question were to be seized and melted down. The 'umper' could even fine those who worked 'openly' in their workshops, lest anyone 'not a member of the fellowship might learn the said occupations and skills'.[4] The 'mystery' of pin-making was further protected by rules against masters working with members of other guilds.

In practice the Pinners' pretentions to full guild status were constantly undermined, both from without and within. The Pinners of London vanish from the record in 1511. For a century or two, however, they nonetheless managed to give their 'mystery' some of the civic and sacred trappings of a guild: candles were burned and Masses said for the Pinners' patron saint; dinners were held and special uniforms purchased for the craft's officers to wear in city processions, whether on land or on hired barges on the Thames. To those on the inside, such guild rituals doubtless made pin-making a noble and distinguished activity. The Scottish pin-makers whom Smith observed at work 250 years later were presumably not members of a guild. They would have struggled to invest the same kind of emotions in the pins that they made. Although Smith is uninterested in the loss of a sense of 'craft', he is very concerned at the harm caused to factory workers by their unrelenting, mind-numbing toil. Though he does not use the term 'alienation', Smith's account of the cost to the labourer of the specialization of labour anticipates that of the nineteenth-century philosopher Karl Marx.

For Smith, guilds are symptomatic of the tendency of men of business to restrict competition, and to lobby the state into protecting them by introducing restrictions on the free market for capital and labour. Like the guild restrictions, these regulations increased prices, lowered quality, discouraged innovation and locked up capital (including human capital, that is, the talents and skills of individuals). Similarly self-serving restrictions on international trade reflected a view of the economy known as mercantilism. Mercantilism encouraged kings and princes to assess the value of their nation's exports and imports, and then intervene in the market to engineer a positive 'balance of trade'. This was done by imposing high tariffs on imports and giving 'bounties' (direct subsidies, tax breaks) or even a monopoly to certain enterprises or certain forms of manufacture in order to increase home production, so as to replace imports and provide new goods to export.

In choosing to interpret Smith's attack on mercantilism as an attack on the state, many capitalists who claim to admire Smith have missed something important. They have also overlooked the even worse things Smith has to say about people like them: men of business who, Smith says, scheme together to create monopolies, and then get the government to support those monopolies and even extend them by military conquest and imperialism. 'People of the same trade seldom meet together, even for merriment and diversion,' Smith notes, 'but the conversation ends in conspiracy against the publick, or in some contrivance to raise prices' (*wn*, 145). While the 'violence and injustice of the rulers of mankind is an ancient evil',

Fibularius. Der Hefftelmacher.

FIbula coccineas quæ stringat eburnea vestes,
    Atq̃ puellarum lactea membra tegat.
Hæc fit ab arte mea, quæ sæpe probatur & ipsis
    Regibus, vt merces has reuerenter emant.

Fibula Reginam torto neq̃ dedecet auro,
    Cùm clamydem nostra fibulat arte suam.
Hæc quoq̃ militibus dabat ornamenta superbis,
    Exbellis olim qui retulêre decus.
Vtitur hac Corydon, hac Thestylis vtitur omnis,
    Arteq̃ rusticitas nescit egere mea.

I 3   Claui.

Jost Amman, 'The Pin Maker', woodcut from *Panoplia omnium illiberalium mechanicarum* [Book of Trades] (1569). Even in 1569 there was some division of labour in pin making: the man makes the pin, his wife puts it in the paper.

one which Smith sees as bound up in an innately human love of tyrannizing, happily he sees no reason why we have to put up with the harmful effects of the businessman's 'monopolizing spirit'. 'The mean rapacity, the monopolizing spirit of merchants and manufacturers, who neither are, nor ought to be the rulers of mankind, though it cannot perhaps be corrected, may very easily be prevented from disturbing the tranquillity of any body but themselves' (*WN*, 493). The price of public tranquillity and economic freedom is eternal vigilance, a healthy distrust of 'men of business'.

A consideration of Smith's thought challenges our preconceived notions of who or what is 'capitalist', in ways that are often surprising. Time after time we find that Smith doesn't persuade us to shift our position on a well-trodden stage, but invites us to change our entire frame of reference. This is especially true of the discipline we call 'economics'. Smith never refers to 'economics' and would not have called himself an 'economist'. The closest he would have come to an economist would have been on his trip to France (1764–6), when he associated with a group of French thinkers led by François Quesnay. This group is usually referred to today as the Physiocrats, but at the time they were sometimes called *les économistes*. Smith's first biographer, Dugald Stewart (1753–1828), claimed that Smith's 'doctrine concerning the freedom of trade and of industry coincides remarkably' with that of the 'French Economists' (*EPS*, 319). Though he wrote about them respectfully, and originally intended to dedicate his *Wealth of Nations* to Quesnay, Smith disagreed with their agriculture-focused concept of the economy. He would not have been very happy to have been called an *économiste* (or even an economist) at the time.

Smith held various academic posts at the University of Glasgow, but they were in logic and moral philosophy, not economics, which did not become a discipline until the late nineteenth century. Moral philosophy fell from favour in the nineteenth century and no longer enjoys the status it had in Smith's day. Trends in higher education and in the way we parcel 'science' into disciplines have left scholars trying to make sense of Smith by using a discipline-specific jargon that only emerged after the eighteenth century – jargon of the sort any scholar today needs to be fluent in if he or she wishes to get an audience, or get promoted. There is a sense in which economists and philosophers engage with 'their Smiths'. Smith himself was well aware that the specialization of labour did not cease to function at the line separating manual labour from brain work. Philosophy and 'speculation' also become particular trades 'in the progress of society' (*wn*, 21).

Thus far we have been making the argument for a more holistic understanding of Smith using stories that have become almost hackneyed as a result of the donkey-work they have been made to do over the years. We trust the reader will permit us to choose a less familiar story: that of 'the poor man's son'. This young man wants to be rich and comes to hate his father's humble cottage, in which he grew up. He believes he would be happier if he had a big house and a grand carriage. Years pass. Through a combination of back-breaking work and by sucking up to the right people, the Poor Man's Son makes it to the top. He's living the dream. Put this way, it is another trite tale, a 'rags-to-riches' yarn we have heard over and over again. But that's not the story Smith tells:

> The poor man's son, whom heaven in its anger has visited with ambition, when he begins to look around him, admires the condition of the rich. He finds the cottage of his father too small for his accommodation, and fancies he should be lodged more at his ease in a palace. He is displeased with being obliged to walk a-foot, or to endure the fatigue of riding on horseback. He sees his superiors carried about in machines, and imagines that in one of these he could travel with less inconveniency. He feels himself naturally indolent, and willing to serve himself with his own hands as little as possible; and judges, that a numerous

retinue of servants would save him from a great deal of trouble. He thinks if he had attained all these, he would sit still and contentedly, and be quiet, enjoying himself in the thought of the happiness and tranquillity of his situation. He is enchanted with the distant idea of this felicity. It appears in his fancy like the life of some superior rank of beings, and, in order to arrive at it, he devotes himself for ever to the pursuit of wealth and greatness. To obtain the conveniencies which these afford, he submits in the first year, nay in the first month of his application, to more fatigue of body and more uneasiness of mind than he could have suffered through the whole of his life from the want of them.

Looking back over his life from near its end, the Poor Man's Son finds all his efforts have been in vain.

Through the whole of his life he pursued the idea of a certain artificial and elegant repose which he may never arrive at, for which he sacrifices a real tranquillity that is at all times in his power, and which, if in the extremity of old age he should at last attain to it, he will find to be in no respect preferable to that humble security and contentment which he had abandoned for it. It is then, in the last dregs of life, his body wasted with toil and diseases, his mind galled and ruffled by the memory of a thousand injuries and disappointments which he imagines he has met with from the injustices of his enemies, or from the perfidy and ingratitude of his friends, that he begins at last to find that wealth and greatness are mere trinkets of frivolous utility, no more adapted for producing ease of body or tranquillity of mind than the tweezer-cases of the lover of toys; and like them too, more troublesome to the person who carries them about with him than all the advantages they can afford him are commodious (*TMS*, 181).

The Apprentice is a popular television programme in which a cast of young go-getters compete for the prize of a job with a six-figure salary and the chance to be mentored by a charismatic businessman – in the British version, the Amstrad pioneer Sir Alan Sugar; in the American one, the property developer Donald Trump. Over several weeks we watch the contestants compete at a series of business-related tasks. Through the hoops they go at breakneck speed, pausing only to preen to camera and vaunt their ruthless business acumen and self-belief. They perform regular obeisances to the far greater acumen of the show's star, a man who appears only at the end of each episode, arriving sometimes by helicopter and sometimes by Rolls-Royce to dispense praise and censure – a plot device used by Greek dramatists and later known in its Latin translation as a *deus ex machina*. The stars' 'palaces' and 'machines' are lovingly depicted, partly (one can't help but suspect) to distract

Though known in French as a *nécessaire*, Smith recognized that the fashion for items like this French tweezer case from *c.* 1765 was about the display of luxury.

from their actual businesses, the precise extent and profitability of which remain obscure.

Each week the winning team is rewarded with a taste of the high-roller lifestyle, which does indeed seem fit for 'a superior race of beings'. One week on the American *Apprentice* the winning team's reward consisted of a tour of Trump's apartment in Trump Tower, in Midtown Manhattan. The usual billing and cooing was interrupted by an unscripted exchange. Standing amid the marble and gold of Trump's dining room, looking out over the breathtaking view, one young would-be apprentice asked when was the last time Trump had dined there. Trump paused. 'That's a good question.' He could not remember. Though this son of a not-so-poor man now had all the 'toys' he could wish for, far from being able to switch to a life of ease (to 'sit still and contentedly, and be quiet') he found himself deprived of one of the simplest and most affordable pleasures: eating with friends.

Is Smith out to spoil our fun? Smith certainly found the values of self-denial and self-command espoused by the Stoic school of ancient Greek philosophy appealing: he calls them 'the best school of heroes and patriots' (*TMS*, 60). Stoics sought to purge themselves of all emotion, reaching a state of complete *apatheia* (from which we get the word apathy), an indifference to life's pleasures as well as its pains. They tended to sneer at those they felt had enslaved themselves to what they considered worthless pursuits of wealth, public esteem and even the most basic comforts. One Stoic, Diogenes of Sinope (412–324 BCE), was famous for living in a jar or barrel and thinking up new and often quite ostentatious ways of living in poverty and showing his disdain for the high and mighty. It is said that, invited to Plato's house for dinner, Diogenes made a point of rubbing his dirty bare feet all over his colleague's fine carpets, commenting, 'I trample on Plato's pride.' 'How much pride you expose to view, Diogenes', his host replied laconically, 'by seeming not to be proud.'[5]

Smith certainly believes that we should restrain our vanity and love of showing off, but he does not believe it is necessary or even virtuous to achieve the Stoics' philosophical detachment from the true happiness derived from love and friendship, or from the duty of care to our reputation, families and financial well-being. He opposed the pessimistic views of human nature popular in his youth, notably those of the German philosopher Samuel von Pufendorf. Pufendorf had been one of the first to attempt to establish the principles of government (a science of politics) on the principles of human nature. Like the Stoics, Pufendorf suspected commerce of encouraging luxury and vanity. While there was room to hope that an educated elite might learn to respect the rules of morality for their own sake, everybody else was to be restrained by fear of God or of the absolute monarchs who ruled in His name.

Smith is not prepared to write off the majority in this way, nor is he prepared to see human emotions as the enemy of human security and society. Smith recognizes that following those emotions can come at a cost. We will be considering the anxiety and alienation which can result, and which are evident in the story of the Poor Man's Son. The Poor Man's Son is deluding himself, but Smith's historical account of the 'progress of opulence' finds similar delusions behind the greatest liberation in the history of western Europe: the transition from feudalism to our commercial society. These delusions have helped impel humankind from the caveman state to the state we are in today, bringing us a vastly improved quality of life as well as freedom from the tyrannical rule of feudal lords and tribal chiefs. Rather than attempting to purge our emotions, Smith wants us to acknowledge, understand and then transcend them.

Smith's own life was uneventful. Born in Kirkcaldy (pronounced 'Ker-cuddy'), a small town on the Firth of Forth in Fife, Scotland, and studied in Glasgow and Oxford. He taught at the University of Glasgow for thirteen years, resigning his

Johann Friedrich Bolt, *Diogenes*, 1799, etching.

chair to head off to France in 1764. After two years in France
and a few months in London he returned to Scotland, and
spent the last twelve years of his life as a customs official back
in Edinburgh. He lived with his mother and never married. His
first biographer, Dugald Stewart, speculates about possible
loves that were not requited. As with the story that has an infant
Smith narrowly escaping kidnap by 'gipsies', however, these
attempts to enliven the narrative of his life are probably just
that.[6] We have few likenesses of the great man. Smith ordered
that all his unpublished notes and drafts be burned after his
death. A bad correspondent who was regularly chaffed by
friends for taking ages to reply, Smith left very few letters behind
for a man of his class and contacts: only 193, a fraction of the
number that survive for other leading thinkers of the day.

Smith was raised a member of 'the Kirk', the Scots Presbyterian Church of Scotland, and had to declare his allegiance to the Church's doctrines before he was permitted to teach. Presbyterianism is a branch of Protestantism that originated in the Scottish Reformation of 1560, which saw Scotland secede from the Roman Catholic Church and the Scottish parliament abolish the jurisdiction of the Pope over church affairs. Subsequent attempts by the Scottish king (from 1603 until 1707 the Scottish and English thrones were officially separate, but held by the same monarch) to bring religious observance and the Church's power structures into line with those of the Church of England led to resistance, however. The Scots wanted their church to be presbyterian (ruled by presbyteries, committees of church elders, who were not priests), not episcopal (ruled by bishops and archbishops). In 1639 resistance became a full-blown civil war, which the king lost. In 1647 the Church of Scotland adopted the Westminster Confession of Faith, a set of statements about God, sin and grace heavily influenced by the sixteenth-century French theologian John Calvin. According to Calvin, each human is either saved by divine grace, or doomed to suffer eternal punishment. Whichever direction it led in, their fate was predetermined by God before the creation of the world. The 'regenerate' (that is, the saved, or 'elect') could not reject divine grace, nor could the 'unregenerate' (the damned) do anything to avoid damnation. Human nature was universally depraved; nothing good could be expected of it without God's direct, miraculous intervention. It was a dour theology.

As a student at the University of Glasgow, however, Smith was heavily influenced by his moral philosophy professor, an Ulster Presbyterian named Francis Hutcheson. Hutcheson formed part of the so-called 'New Light' movement within Presbyterianism, which sought to soften this harsh image of humanity as innately, irredeemably bad. Rather than being vile and ignorant insects, humans had been created by God with certain desires that led them to recognize good behaviour and find it pleasing in itself, rather than simply as a means to escape eternal punishment. Hutcheson faced strong criticism from 'Old Light' Presbyterians, who accused him of heresy. They were concerned that Hutcheson was shifting the terms of discussion about right and wrong behaviour from a theological discussion about grace and sin to a philosophical, secular one about virtue and vice. Sin and grace were mysterious forces that mortals could neither influence nor understand. To be right was simply to obey the will of God, which in any case was not really a choice as far as Calvinists were concerned. To discuss virtue and vice was to join a debate that pre-dated Christ's entry into the world, with the writings of ancient Greeks such as Aristotle, Plato and Socrates, and which was suspect for that very reason. All who lived before Christ had obviously not received grace and were in Hell, so why on earth would one listen to them? Those thinkers had attempted to find a basis for morality founded on human, rather than divine, judgement. That was both foolish and sinfully presumptuous.

Hutcheson argued that the study of human nature revealed not a seething chaos of sin, but a divinely created mechanism of 'springs' (desires, instincts), which were designed to lead humans towards sociable and good behaviour. This mechanism was aesthetically pleasing, God had intended us to find it a pleasure to contemplate, as a further encouragement to right behaviour. Provided we continued to view these 'springs' as divine in nature and the universe as designed with a certain goal, the discussion of sin and grace and that of virtue and vice could run in parallel. Admittedly, to many Christians (Presbyterians or not) this approach remained worrying because it involved looking at the world rather than sacred texts – that is, sidelining revelation. Rather than taking our conception of good behaviour from direct communication with God (revelation, as given to certain prophets who subsequently handed the message down through sacred texts), Hutcheson looked to the world around him for clues and sought to understand the lessons of God through them.

This science of working out the nature of God by studying the nature of Creation was called 'natural theology', a subject that Smith would later give lectures on. Smith regularly describes this or that emotion as implanted in us by 'Nature', that is, by the Creator. He certainly believed that these emotions were implanted with a kindly purpose in mind, that the universe was designed to develop certain qualities and even a particular kind of society. But Smith's reluctance to use the word 'God' and the entire absence of any reference to Jesus (a figure even some non-Christians cherish as a moral teacher) leave us in the dark about whose 'mind' this was. As a professor and public figure, however, Smith paid respect to the status quo and was nervous of being tarred with the anti-clerical views of his friend David Hume, a philosopher whom many contemporaries reviled as little better than an atheist. It is difficult for us today to grasp just how seriously this label was taken in Smith's day, when belief in a personalized deity was universal. At that time, atheists were abhorrent and truly frightening figures, a source of contagion that endangered anyone who came into contact with them.

Presbyterian attitudes and institutions were changing, therefore, during Smith's lifetime. So too were Scottish ones, dramatically so during the six years he spent studying at Oxford in the 1740s. The 1707 Act of Union had made Scotland and England (and Wales) one kingdom, with a single parliament sitting in London. Until the 2014 referendum on Scottish independence the ever-closer union of England and Scotland as allied elements of Great Britain seemed natural, the benefits to both parties self-evident, and therefore largely unstated. In Smith's day this consensus was still in the process of formation, though Smith was convinced that 'the Union was a measure from which infinite Good has been derived to this country' (*c*, 68). In 1745, while Smith was still in Oxford, a rival,

Roman Catholic claimant to the British throne, Charles Edward Stuart (the Young Pretender, also known as Bonnie Prince Charlie), left exile in France and staged a campaign to unseat King George II, son of George I, the Protestant Hanoverian monarch who had been placed on the British throne by Parliament in 1714.

Charles landed in Scotland, raised an army from among the Highland clans who still professed loyalty to the House of Stuart, and marched south into England. After causing panic in London and across England, Charles lost his nerve and retreated, his forces ruthlessly defeated by the English army at the Battle of Culloden in April 1746. Smith was not a Jacobite; that is, one of those seeking to replace the Hanoverians with the Stuarts. For him, the economic and cultural benefits of the union were self-evident – so much so that he rarely felt the need to articulate them. Even before 'the Forty-five', Smith's Kirkcaldy accent would nonetheless have brought unwelcome attention south of the border, and he presumably learned to soften his accent while at Oxford. After the accession of King George III to the British throne in 1760 it was rumoured that a new, more successful invasion was under way. Supposedly encouraged by George's highly unpopular prime minister, Lord Bute (a Scot), hordes of poor Scots were (it was said) heading to London in order to steal jobs that rightfully belonged to Englishmen.

For all their education and talent, Scots like Smith needed to watch their backs in England, and they tended to stick together in places like London, where they convened in the British Coffeehouse near Charing Cross. This arguably fuelled a sense among the English of the Scots as a canny coterie weaselling their way into positions of power within a rapidly expanding British empire. Far from masterminding a Scottish conquest of England, however, Smith and the other luminaries of the Scottish Enlightenment were enthusiastic participants in a mutually improving dialogue intended to foster 'Improvement' in Scotland. As a young man Smith himself benefited from reforms of the University of Glasgow

Earthenware punch bowl with portrait of Charles Edward Stuart, 1749. Smith would not have joined in with those who toasted 'Bonnie Prince Charlie' using punch bowls like this.

that were intended to make it a forcing-house for a more aristocratic and 'polite' elite, rather than merely a seminary for Presbyterian churchmen. Where previously they were largely content to run their estates as their forefathers had, thanks to this spirit of 'Improvement', landowners such as Smith's patron, the Duke of Buccleuch, were experimenting with new farming methods, new transport infrastructure (canals), new means of production (factories, rather than small workshops) and new ways of financing them (banks).

Although it brought mixed results to Smith's hometown (Kirkcaldy lies on the east coast), the shift in trade from the North

Sea (the Dutch Republic and the Baltic) to the Atlantic trade (the Caribbean and the North American colonies) greatly enriched Glasgow in the eighteenth century. Together with the military defeat of the 'savage' clans of the Highlands in 'the Forty-five', these dramatic changes made Glasgow and Scotland an object lesson in what we would call 'development', one to which Smith paid close attention. These changes would not have come about without the 1707 Act of Union.

Smith's expedition to France in 1764–6 as tutor to the son of the Duke of Buccleuch gave Smith his only experience of foreign travel apart from these trips to England. Introduced by Hume, then working in Paris as secretary to the British ambassador, Smith circulated among the salons of the great *philosophes* of the Enlightenment. Locked together by ties of history, repeated wars and mutual fascination for each other's literature and fashions, the leading minds of Britain and France communicated frequently in this period, and Smith's works were soon translated into French, helping to compensate for Smith's poor command of spoken French. Though Smith engaged with the thought of French and Swiss philosophers such as Quesnay and Jean-Jacques Rousseau, it was Smith's friendship with David Hume (twelve years older), a fellow Scot, that had the deepest impact on his thought. Exactly when they first met is unknown, but 1750 seems a reasonable guess. In the 1750s Hume published a number of essays that anticipated some of Smith's later arguments, such as those discussing what Hume called 'the jealousy of trade', the beggar-thy-neighbour views of mercantilism, which sees all trade as a zero-sum game. Hume's atheism tested this friendship and confronted Smith with some tricky personal and professional dilemmas.

Though less outspoken than Hume, Smith's wide range of interests, intelligence and dry sense of humour clearly won the affection of his students, and his surviving works relay a lively sense of his speaking style and delivery. Though the focus here will

A glass paste medallion of Adam Smith, by James Tassie, 1787.

be on his thought, it is important not to lose sight of this context, or of the ways in which Smith's rhetoric supports his arguments. *The Theory of Moral Sentiments*, for example, lacks many of the features normally found in philosophical treatises: there is no introduction laying out the plan of the work, very few footnotes and few references to other philosophers before we get to Part VII (266 pages into a 342-page work). Rather than fencing with other philosophers, Smith preferred to appeal to his reader's own experience. As we have seen already, he also liked to use examples drawn from everyday life. As Smith's friend and contemporary, the politician and thinker Edmund Burke, noted in a review for the *Annual Register*, 'The illustrations are numerous and happy, and shew the author to be a man of uncommon observation. His language is easy and spirited, and puts things before you in the fullest light; it is rather painting than writing.'[7]

This book is divided into six chapters, organized around key Smithian concepts, but also following Smith's life and times. Such an approach is possible thanks to our subject's precociousness: Smith developed the broad outlines of his moral philosophy early on, and the rest of his life was largely a matter of making refinements and experimenting with different means of persuasion. The first chapter considers Smith's childhood, education and career up to his appointment to the Glasgow chair in 1751. Chapter Two covers the 1750s, and introduces Smith's concepts of sympathy and the passions, which together make up the ethics advanced in the *Theory of Moral Sentiments*. The following chapter considers Smith's trip to Paris as a tutor, contrasting his historical account of the development of society with that advanced by Rousseau. On his return from France Smith returned to Kirkcaldy to work on the *The Wealth of Nations*. Chapter Four considers the interplay between the arguments advanced in that work and the economic and imperial crises experienced in Scotland and the wider British empire during these years.

The success of the *The Wealth of Nations* led to Smith's appointment in 1778 as Commissioner of Customs and his move to Edinburgh. Struggling with the competing demands of his writing and his customs work, and mourning the loss of his beloved mother Margaret, Smith curtailed his writing programme in order to focus on a thorough revision of the *Theory of Moral Sentiments*. The conclusion considers these revisions, bringing us full circle. After considering how Smith's model of justice is viewed today, it invites the reader to think upon Smith's achievement of transcending moral philosophy and political economy as offering nothing less than a model of human behaviour – a way to balance our limitations and our potential, to combine 'the best heart' with 'the best head' (*TMS*, 216).

1

The Theatre of Nature, 1723–50

Philosophers are made, not born – at least, according to Smith. As he writes in *The Theory of Moral Sentiments*, a philosopher and 'a common street porter' might display 'the most dissimilar characters', but the apparent differences in personality, income and talent result 'not so much from nature, as from habit, custom, and education'. As children, he notes, it would have been hard for their respective parents or playmates to see any difference between them. They were two boys like any others. One boy did not become a philosopher because of his extraordinary brain, nor did the other become a porter because he had been born with especially strong muscles suitable for carrying things around. The philosopher might subsequently deny this natural resemblance, insisting that he had become a philosopher because he was more intelligent than the porter. But that is just vanity.

It also reflects our desire to identify an aesthetically pleasing efficiency or fitness (what Smith calls 'propriety') in the way our society assigns men and women to different ranks and professions. It does not just hurt our pride, after all, to be told that our choice of career was the result of a series of accidents, chiefly of birth (in Smith's day, as in ours, the main determinant of a child's future income was its parents' income, not its own 'genius' or intelligence). It induces anxiety by suggesting that our society is not as ordered as we desire it to appear. We like to think that the philosopher and the porter rightly belong in their respective

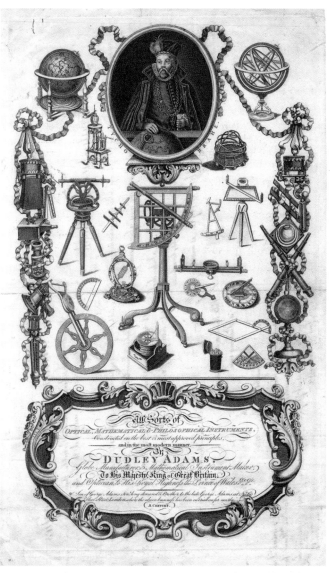

An eighteenth-century trade card advertising the scientific instrument maker Dudley Adams.

positions in society. Together this vanity and this appetite for systems lead us to confuse causes with effects. 'The difference of natural talents in different men is, in reality, much less than we are aware of,' Smith notes, 'and the very different genius which appears to distinguish men of different professions, when grown up to maturity, is not upon many occasions so much as the cause, as the effect of the division of labour' (*WN*, 28). The porter has strong muscles because after boyhood he was set to work carrying things. Had he been given a different education and set to reading books, he would not have developed the muscles that made him appear a born porter. In considering Adam Smith's early life, it does indeed seem as if 'habit, custom and education' played a greater role than 'nature'.

Adam Smith was born in the summer of 1723 in the Scottish port town of Kirkcaldy, which lies on the east coast, on the opposite side of the river Forth from the Scottish capital, Edinburgh. Today Kirkcaldy has a population of 46,000, largely supported by linoleum production. In Smith's youth, however, its population was much smaller, and it may well have seemed as if the town's heyday was long past. Kirkcaldy had won the right to hold a market in 1334. It gained administrative independence in 1644 when King Charles I made it a royal burgh. This status released it from the financial burdens and legal jurisdiction of the local feudal landlord, the abbot of Dunfermline. Elsewhere in Scotland, notably among the Highland clans, this medieval system of feudal land tenure continued into Smith's day and beyond. Once free from these feudal ties, Kirkcaldy expanded as a port and trading centre, thriving on the North Sea trade, especially with the Netherlands. In the eighteenth century, however, the commercial tide turned from east to west, from the North Sea to the Atlantic, and from the trade in salt and coal to the trade in tobacco, sugar and other products exported to Glasgow (on the west side of Scotland) from Britain's rapidly expanding colonies in North America.

The 1707 union of the monarchies of Scotland and England also led to increased taxation. Seven years later the British parliament sitting in London placed a German princeling (George, Elector of Hanover) on the British throne. King George I had few ties to Britain and did not even speak English, but was at least Protestant, like the vast majority of his new subjects. In placing George on the throne Parliament had had to jump over many other men with far stronger claims, but who were disqualified on the grounds of being Roman Catholic. The lead claimant (or pretender), James Edward Stuart, led his Scottish supporters in a revolt in 1715. Though unsuccessful, this insurrection brought further disruption and taxation to Kirkcaldy. Between 1655 and 1755 the population more than halved, to 2,296.

Smith would live to see this process begin to go into reverse, however, as Kirkcaldy turned from trade to manufacturing. Local supplies of timber and the port made shipbuilding a profitable endeavour, and nail-making was an established industry. Flax was imported from the Netherlands and the Baltic for working into linen, not in large mills but rather through cottage industry: under the 'putting out system', tenant farmers contracted with linen 'factors' (manufacturers) to produce linen on a piecework basis, being supplied with flax which they worked into linen on a loom at home. Annual Scottish linen output increased from 5.5 million yards to 13.5 million between 1746 and 1771.[1] Later on, stocking manufacture was introduced to the area. The creation of linen floorcloths in the following century laid the foundations of the city's linoleum boom. The immediate surroundings of Kirkcaldy were a mixed economy; alongside sheep-herding, forestry and agriculture there was proto-industrialization (the putting out system), industrialization (the nail works, the shipyards) and both local and international trade. What Kirkcaldy lacked in fine architecture it more than made up for in the range of economic activities it supported. Smith's father was well placed to observe all this activity – indeed, it was his duty to do so – as a Kirkcaldy customs officer.

Unfortunately, Adam Smith never knew his father. Adam Smith senior, at the age of 44, died five months before his son was born. There were no siblings, apart from a half-brother, Hugh, the product of Adam Smith senior's first marriage. Hugh was fourteen years older and probably also worked in the customs service – the customs were something of a family business, with other Smiths working for the customs in Alloa, Montrose and Aberdeen.[2] Hugh and Adam had little contact. Even if they never met, the two Adam Smiths' careers were surprisingly similar: both served as customs officials and both relied on a network of aristocratic patronage. The elder Smith was secretary to the third Earl of Loudoun, whose support doubtless helped him secure his appointment in 1714 as Controller of Customs in Kirkcaldy; other members of the Smith family worked in a similar capacity for the Duke of Argyll, an even more powerful Scottish landowner. Marriage to the daughter of another landowner and Member of Parliament in 1720 further boosted Adam Smith senior's fortunes and network of contacts. Young Adam Smith was set to inherit a comfortable estate as well as these contacts, who served as guardians of his property until he came of age and was legally able to administer it himself.

'Habits and customs' of patronage thus linked father and son in service to a particular segment of the traditional Scottish landowning aristocracy. These earls and dukes supported the union of 1707 rather than the Jacobites. The Hereditable Jurisdictions (Scotland) Act of 1746 stripped them and their peers of their remaining legal powers. But union with England did not just take, it also gave. In a process of co-option by the monarchy these noblemen's support of the Union was rewarded. The British monarchy compensated them with new forms of patronage, with powers to nominate their retainers to new state offices in the customs service, in the courts and elsewhere. These noblemen's dress, accent and manners gradually became more English, and some settled south of the border on a near-permanent basis. Many looked to England for the resources in capital and know-how they felt were necessary for the economic development of Scotland. By the 1770s the obscure dialect, dress and particularly the poetic traditions of the Highlands were beginning to appear quaint and desirably authentic, laying the foundations of that romantic image of Scotland that underpins today's tourist industry. In the 1720s, however, they simply seemed barbaric and threatening (because of their Jacobitism). A new agenda of 'Improvement' was born, which sought to strike a balance between innovation and a patriotic respect for native institutions. Both Smiths played a part in this project, which they certainly would not have seen as compromising their Scottish identity.

But alongside 'habits and customs' such as patronage and patriotism, 'education' was equally important in shaping the younger Smith's development. Smith's mother Margaret would have taken the first steps, forging a mother–son bond that proved exceptionally strong. In 1723 Kirkcaldy's town council had built a two-room school, which remained in use until 1843. The system of parish schools found across Scotland as well as the universities reflected a widespread respect for education, sufficient to lead almost all Scottish parents to make the financial and other sacrifices (such as the loss of their child's labour – a valuable commodity in itself) necessary to send their children to school for a few years. In school Smith not only learned reading, writing and arithmetic but Latin and some Greek. In *The Wealth of Nations* Smith argues that this grammar school curriculum, which saw 'the children of common people' taught 'a little smattering of Latin', should be replaced with one with space for 'the elementary parts of geometry and mechanicks'. As he noted, few trades demanded Latin, whereas 'there is scarce a common trade which does not afford some opportunities of applying to it the principles of geometry and mechanicks' (*WN*, 785–6).

Latin and Greek allowed the young Smith to read classical philosophical and historical texts in the original language. Indeed, that was the whole point to teaching these dead languages: to gain access to a classical world whose art and rhetoric were held to embody the greatest that human culture could achieve; whose philosophers, statesmen and military leaders eclipsed anything the modern world had to offer. Having recovered this culture in the Renaissance of the fifteenth century, in the eighteenth century western Europe was only just beginning to think that the moderns might in fact outdo the ancients. Smith may have been exposed to the thought of Stoic philosophers while still at Kirkcaldy: an eighteenth-century edition of the *Encheiridion* (Handbook, compiled by Epictetus' pupil Arrian) survives with Smith's name on it, and may date from his youth there.

The *Encheiridion* teaches us to rid ourselves of the fantasy that we have power over our bodies, possessions or other external things, when we only have power to control our inner state. We achieve true freedom or tranquillity (in Greek, *ataraxia*) through self-knowledge, silencing the desires that threaten to enslave us, and achieving command over our emotions (*apatheia*). We are then free to act as 'a member of the vast commonwealth of nature' (*TMS*, 140). The Stoics were often contrasted with the Epicurean school, which also emerged in third-century BCE Greece, but which Smith would have known mainly through the writings of the first-century BCE Roman poet Lucretius. Epicureans teach that humans achieve *ataraxia* through the pursuit of pleasure. Though the word 'epicurean' was and is often used to refer to individuals who see pleasure as the highest good (hedonists) and supposedly indulge in orgies of various kinds, true Epicureans recognize the pains of over-indulgence (hangovers, STDs, self-loathing) and hence seek pleasure in moderation. They seek a form of government founded on an 'original contract', which protects the members of society from harm and allows them to pursue pleasure.

Epictetus, Lucretius and other great philosophers of antiquity were lifelong companions for Smith, and university gave him further opportunities to study their teachings. In 1737 Smith left his hometown and entered the University of Glasgow. It was not unusual for boys to attend university at such an age. Thanks to the aforementioned trade in tobacco with the colonies across the Atlantic, Glasgow was a growing city, albeit half the size of Edinburgh, with a population of 23,500 in 1755. Today the university is based in a Victorian suburb of the city, in a large Gothic Revival complex. In Smith's day the university was in the city's heart, built around two Georgian quadrangles with a pleasant garden. Here Smith remained for three years, attending lectures on logic, Latin, Greek, moral philosophy, natural philosophy and mathematics. The majority of these would have been delivered in Latin, and all would have commenced with a prayer. Until 1726 the university smacked of a seminary, primarily intended to train priests for ordination in the Church of Scotland. The creation of new chairs in logic, moral philosophy and natural philosophy in that year formed part of an attempt to broaden the university's appeal, attracting the sons of the merchant and aristocratic elite, for whom paying lecture fees was no hardship but who did not plan to spend their lives in the pulpit or the law courts. Rather than providing an apprenticeship for a guild of priests or lawyers, the Scottish universities increasingly sought to provide an education, a set of tools for thinking and discussing. This learning was defined as 'polite' rather than narrowly 'useful'.

We know very little about Smith's first Glasgow period, but he clearly learned much from the professor of moral philosophy, Francis Hutcheson. Born in County Down in Northern Ireland, Hutcheson had come to the University of Glasgow in 1710, aged sixteen. After establishing an academy in Dublin and publishing his *Inquiry into the Original of our Ideas of Beauty and Virtue* (1725) he returned to Glasgow to take up his chair in 1730, delivering his inaugural lecture on 'the social nature of man'. Though this

lecture was delivered and published in Latin, Hutcheson otherwise
fully supported the aforementioned project to modernize the
university's curriculum. He was the first professor at Glasgow
to switch to lecturing in English and was rewarded with large
audiences. But his 'New Light' views on the innate goodness
of man angered orthodox Presbyterians. He seemed to suggest
that humans could work their own salvation without turning to
Jesus Christ, God's only son, who had been sent to bring humans
salvation by offering himself as the one perfect sacrifice for their
sin. A year into Smith's time at Glasgow, Hutcheson was hauled
before the Church elders and charged with deviating from the
1647 Westminster Confession, the basis of Church of Scotland
orthodoxy. Though he was not convicted, it doubtless provided
his student Smith with a lesson in the need for public instructors
to exercise professional prudence. In 1743 Hutcheson's ally,
professor of divinity William Leechman, was prosecuted for
heresy, using information gathered by student informants.

The University of Glasgow in Smith's day. John Slezer, 'The Colledge of Glasgow',
engraving from *Theatrum Scotiae* (1697).

In his *Inquiry* and his inaugural lecture Hutcheson tackled those philosophers and moralists who saw humans' passionate nature as making 'the state of nature' a miserable state of wanton violence. By 'state of nature' these thinkers were referring to a pre-social state, to the behaviour of humans before certain rules were laid down (in an 'original contract') and they entered a properly regulated society. For Thomas Hobbes in *Leviathan* (1651) human life in this state was 'solitary, poor, nasty, brutish, and short'. Hobbes in turn influenced Samuel von Pufendorf, who, while little read today, was one of the most influential philosophers in early eighteenth-century Europe. Pufendorf's *De officio hominis et civis* (1673) was translated into English in 1691 by Andrew Tooke as *The Whole Duty of Man According to the Law of Nature*. At least 145 other editions and translations appeared in the years to 1789. Pufendorf argued that humans acted virtuously only out of fear of divine punishment and the expectation of divine reward. Were this God-focused hope and fear to be removed, 'no Man would be found that would do Works of *Charity* or of *Friendship*, except with probable Expectation of Glory or Profit'.[3]

Without God, we would only ever act after first considering if our action served our own interest. This argument was taken to its logical conclusion by Bernard Mandeville in *The Fable of the Bees* (1714). In rhyming couplets Mandeville presents a 'Paradise' of plenty and wealth, in which all humans act only out of a regard for self-interest. When 'vice' is taken away and replaced by 'virtue', the plenty and wealth disappear. Now that everyone is content with what they have rather than constantly chasing after luxuries, development ceases. Even charitable activity stops, because, Mandeville insists, charitable acts are only performed from a desire for praise. 'Private vice, publick benefits' neatly sums up Mandeville's argument, which shocked contemporaries as exemplifying the depravity that inevitably resulted when philosophical speculation was allowed to get out of hand.

In his inaugural lecture Hutcheson took these thinkers to task for their use of the expression 'state of nature'. It was a 'highly objectionable abuse' to set this supposed state in opposition to 'civil society' and to exclude from it 'everything that is produced by human powers' and as a result of 'natural appetites'. As well as being a 'slander on human nature', this was 'an impiety against our heavenly Father', who, after all, created humans with those same 'powers' and 'appetites':

> If we are to care at all about our use of words, the 'state of nature' ought to denote either that condition to which men are for the most part brought through the exercise of all the natural appetites and powers, or else that most perfect condition to which men can rise by the most sagacious use of all their powers and faculties, a use that seems to be enjoined by the innate desire for the greatest happiness and by whatever benevolent and kind affections that may be natural to man.

While 'certain parts of our nature and certain appetites' led us into vices 'in this fallen state' (a reference to the biblical Fall), when we consider 'the entire structure of human nature', our 'public and benevolent affections' and our 'moral sense that we also call natural conscience, we also see clearly that the vices do not belong to our nature; and we discern those parts that ought to restrain and govern the lower appetites.'[4] In his *Essay on the Nature and Conduct of the Passions and Affections, with Illustrations on the Moral Sense* (1728) Hutcheson developed this 'conscience' into a 'sense', arguing that in addition to our five 'external senses' (sight, touch and so on) humans also have a range of other senses: an 'internal sense', a 'publick sense' (by which we shared in the happiness and misery of others) and a 'moral sense', by which we perceive '*Virtue*, or *Vice* in our selves, and others'.[5] By means of this last sense we are able to feel virtue and vice in others and in ourselves, without any apparent need for thought or reflection.

Far from our love of society deriving from a desire to use others as instruments in service of our own interest (including our own safety), Hutcheson pointed out that humans seek the company of other humans for its own sake. This truth is, of course, obvious, and Hutcheson felt embarrassed at stating something obvious. Yet, as he pointed out, philosophers including Hobbes and Pufendorf had overlooked this entirely. The medieval scholastic philosophers, he noted, sought to understand 'the *Summum Bonum*' (the highest good), but indulged in flights of abstraction that left the common man far behind. 'They seldom mention the delights of humanity, good nature, kindness, mutual love, friendships', he noted; 'They scarce ever spend a word upon the earthly subjects of laborious diligence in some honest employment.' Their abstraction in turn encouraged 'later moralists' (like Mandeville, presumably) to leave out of their own systems 'all enquiries into happiness'. Rather than considering how humans felt, they spoke exclusively of the 'external advantages of peace and wealth'. This was a serious omission, 'since amidst peace and wealth, there may be sullenness, discontent, fretfulness, and all the miseries of poverty'.[6]

Hutcheson's lectures encouraged Smith to view human nature as a worthy focus of study, as something with its own 'structure' rather than something 'fallen' and thereby condemned to sinful disorder. This 'structure' was made up of a variety of 'springs', 'appetites' and 'parts': Hutcheson saw 'reason' and a 'moral sense' as examples of these, along with 'interest' (the care of our own well-being, including financial well-being) and the 'passions' (emotions). There was a hierarchy to these 'parts'. There was also a 'wonderful natural contagiousness' that led us naturally to share our joys with other humans.[7] This sympathy would take centre stage in Smith's thought, as would Hutcheson's aforementioned observation that 'peace and wealth' can be bought at the cost of tranquillity. Hutcheson also anticipated Smith in denying the existence of any 'original contract'. A reverence for the divine intelligence Hutcheson identified in human nature was, perhaps, a sop to his devout listeners, who clearly noticed that divine reward and punishment were far less prominent than they had been for Pufendorf. Above all, Hutcheson taught Smith to keep his feet on the ground, to find explanations that worked for 'earthly subjects' like you and I, and not to lose sight of the common sources of human pleasure (tranquillity, friendship), let alone sacrifice them in the pursuit of economic development. It is not enough to be good and to have the means of happiness; we have to cultivate our human nature so that we actually feel good and are happy.

Smith must have performed well academically in these years, because in 1740 he was awarded a scholarship. The Snell Exhibition had been endowed to allow those intending to become priests to study at Balliol College, Oxford. There was a hefty £500 (around £43,000 today) penalty in place to recoup funds from winners who received such support but subsequently failed to enter the Church. By Smith's day, however, this was no longer enforced, and there is no evidence that Smith ever intended to become a priest. On the contrary, his writings can seem reluctant to discuss or even name God, preferring to use terms such as the 'the Author of nature' (*TMS*, 77). Jesus is never named. Unfortunately we know almost nothing about what Smith did during his six years in Oxford. When *The Theory of Moral Sentiments* was published in 1759 a friend wrote to Smith of the warm reception of his work on both sides of the Scottish border: 'It comforts the English a good deal to hear that you were bred at Oxford, they claim some part of you on that account' (*c*, 40).

Smith himself did not acknowledge this intellectual paternity, and was highly critical of Oxford in *The Wealth of Nations*, in which he discusses the best ways of funding universities. If professors enjoyed an endowed income (rather than, as in Scotland, deriving part of their income from student fees) and were allowed to govern themselves, the outcome was clear: all professors would neglect their duty. 'In the university of Oxford,' Smith observed, 'the greater part of the publick professors have, for these many years, given up altogether even the pretence of teaching' (*WN*, 761). Smith's account is supported by other sources, indicating that the university reached an intellectual nadir in the mid-eighteenth century. The Jacobite politics of the college would have made Balliol particularly unappealing to Smith, who remained in Oxford throughout the second Jacobite rebellion in 1745. Outside Balliol, Smith would have suffered from the hostile English view of Scottish migrants as uncouth, barbarian carpetbaggers. Other than providing the opportunity to soften his Scottish accent, therefore, Oxford's only service to Smith lay in its libraries. Smith's extensive knowledge of ancient and modern history, the natural sciences, of the theatre as well as of poetry and even the romantic fiction of Samuel Richardson and Pierre de Marivaux was doubtless laid down during his six long years of reading in Oxford.

Richardson's novels were the best-sellers of Smith's student years. Before Richardson, novels or 'romances' had been associated with tall tales of fictional kings and queens in far-off lands and were accused of having a corrupting influence on young, impressionable readers, particularly young girls. *Pamela* (1740) and *Clarissa* (1748), by contrast, were set in contemporary England, a world familiar not only to English readers, but to readers across Europe. The French philosopher Denis Diderot's 1762 eulogy of Richardson nicely captures this wonder at fiction's power to help readers understand lived experience:

This author does not send blood flowing down the walls, he does not transport you to distant lands, he does not expose you to being eaten by savages, he does not confine himself within the secret haunts of debauchery, he never wanders off into the world

Vous m'avez donné la vie, oh Madame!
n'en rendez pas le reste misérable.

An illustration by Rémi Delvaux after Clément-Pierre Marillier, from a 1783
French edition of Samuel Richardson's novel *Clarissa*.

of fantasy. The world we live in is his scene of action, his drama is anchored in truth, his people are as real as it is possible to be, his characters are taken from the world of society, his events belong to the customs of all civilized nations; the passions he portrays are those I feel within me; the same things arouse them, and I recognize their force in myself; the problems and afflictions of his people are of the same kind as those which constantly hang over me; he shows me the general course of life as I experience it.[8]

Richardson's transformation of the novel genre anticipated Smith's transformation of the genre of philosophical treatise in *The Theory of Moral Sentiments*. Like Richardson's fiction, Smith's sentimental moral philosophy is intended to address 'the world we live in' and dissect 'the passions I feel within me'.

It may have been in Oxford that Smith first drafted the text we know under the title 'History of Astronomy', a text Smith considered important enough to spare it from the flames in 1790. The 'History' considers 'all the different systems of nature' that have been adopted in the 'western parts of the world'. Rather than constructing this history as a narrative of progress from darkness, superstition and ignorance to Enlightenment and truth, Smith instead puts truth and truth claims entirely to one side. He is interested only in 'how far each [system] was fitted to sooth the imagination, and to render the theatre of nature a more coherent, and therefore a more magnificent spectacle, than otherwise it would have appeared to be' (*EPS*, 46). He is not concerned with judgements as to which model is real; indeed, Smith never shows much interest in 'this cobweb science of Ontology', that is, the study of the nature of being and reality (*WN*, 771). The 'History' does not consider science in positivist terms, as a series of ever-more accurate approximations to reality, but as the product of a desire to impose order on the impressions we receive through our senses and the ideas we derive from them.

Far from being the product of a specific moment in history (an 'Age of Enlightenment', say) and a specific culture (that of 'civilized' western Europe), this desire was present at all times, in all parts of the world. The 'History' notes an overarching pattern, whereby the mental 'machines' we build as models of the universe become simpler over time; polytheistic world views that have several different gods or systems of physics based on multiple forces are simplified. Of course, these machines are so extensive that they embrace wide expanses of human thought. Indeed, they encompass fields of thought that many today consider mutually exclusive – they include theology as well as the natural sciences. But even within the academic disciplines of moral philosophy or economics Smith recognized how the 'love of system' can lead us to oversimplify or pervert the truth in seeking to rebuild the universe around a pet notion or concept.

Coherence is not something that is waiting to be discovered in nature. Coherence and order are imposed onto nature, to turn something confusing or frightening into something 'coherent' and 'magnificent'. Although none of his writings on the subject survive, Smith seems to have had a deep interest in botany, and so it is unsurprising that the 'History' considers other natural sciences apart from astronomy, discussing taxonomy, the classificatory systems by which men of science organize life forms. The Linnaean binomial system of classifying living things (by which we know humans as *Homo sapiens*), for example, involves grouping all creatures into kingdoms, phyla, classes, orders, families, genera and species, thus rendering a cloud of infinitely varied organisms as a neat tree-shaped diagram. This 'nature' is not nature itself, but our human model of it. As Smith says, we are ultimately performing nature in 'the theatre of nature', not in nature itself. What do we do, Smith asks, when we discover a new creature that does not fit into our classificatory tree, or (to return to astronomy) if we discover a new planet whose orbit does not fit our model of the solar system? Do we immediately pull our model apart and start over again, like the good scientists we claim to be?

Of course not, Smith replies. The man of science usually opts to stretch his model so as to squeeze in the inconvenient discovery, or else dismisses the creature or observation as a 'Play of Nature' – in other words, as a one-off (*EPS*, 40). If we believe ourselves to be close to completing a jigsaw puzzle and suddenly find a piece down the back of the sofa that just doesn't fit, most of us will behave similarly: either we mash the piece into the last available space, or quietly 'lose' it again. Nicolaus Copernicus's model of the solar system gave way to that of Johannes Kepler, who made several observations of planetary motion that Copernicus's model could not explain. As Smith notes, most astronomers preferred to cling to the Copernican consensus rather than accept the evidence of their senses (in this case, what their eyes were seeing). They put 'the coherence of the ideas of their imagination' first (*EPS*, 77). Far from hailing Kepler's discoveries as an opportunity to improve their system, they found them a source of embarrassment (*EPS*, 86). Though Smith is rarely given much credit by historians or philosophers of science, the sophistication of Smith's understanding of the nature of discovery (rather than the discovery of nature) is striking. A century later, the reception of Charles Darwin's radical rearrangement of the Linnaean tree as a historical pedigree would be met with rather more embarrassment than enthusiasm.

In 1746 Smith returned to Kirkcaldy, near enough to Edinburgh to join in the city's thriving intellectual and cultural life, focused around new societies and institutions such as the Philosophical Society, the Select Society and the Edinburgh Society for Encouraging Arts, Sciences, Manufactures and Agriculture in Scotland. Although the exact timing of their first meeting is unclear, Smith's closest friendship, that with David Hume, had its origins around this time, in the years between Smith's return from England and his appointment to the University of Glasgow in 1751. Hume had been born and educated in Edinburgh, and came from a similar social background. After suffering a breakdown of some sort, Hume moved to Bristol and then France, where he wrote *A Treatise of Human Nature*, published anonymously in two parts in 1739 and 1740. The *Treatise* was succeeded by volumes of *Essays, Moral and Political*, published in 1741–2. Hume had a strong sense of his own philosophical vocation – stronger than Smith's – and an equally strong sense of entitlement in seeking the financial independence he felt necessary to achieve his revolutionary aim: to establish nothing less than a 'science of man' intended to support all other sciences, one founded on experience and observation. Scandalously, Hume included 'natural religion' among these sciences. Like everything else – even our sense of self and our own mind – this religion was to be constructed from nothing but the 'impressions' given to our mind by our emotions and our senses, and the 'ideas', that is, the images of these 'impressions' that we manipulate in our minds when we think.

Hume's understanding of human nature was similar to Hutcheson's, as were his dismissive views of earlier systems of morality and the 'original contract'. Hume saw himself as a 'metaphysician' rather than 'moralist', however. In a letter of 1739 to Hutcheson, Hume sought to defend himself against the charge of insufficient 'warmth in the cause of virtue', arguing that 'any warm sentiment of morals, I am afraid, would have the air of declamation amidst abstract reasonings.' He added, however, that he intended 'to make a new trial' and see 'if it be possible to make the moralist and metaphysician agree a little better'. Hume argued that the connection between cause and effect could never be discovered, and the apparent necessity linking them was nothing but the effect 'of custom on the imagination'; if past experience had led us to associate 'cause' with a certain 'effect', then it was probable (but not certain) that a similar cause would have a similar effect.[9] 'I cannot agree to your sense of natural', his letter to Hutcheson continued, 'It is founded on final causes; which is a consideration, that appears to me pretty uncertain and unphilosophical.'[10] Hume thus disposed of causality as a basis for his natural religion, including God himself, the First Cause. This, combined with his 'want of warmth', lent him a reputation for unorthodoxy that prevented him from securing Edinburgh's chair in moral philosophy in 1744. It was, after all, one of the responsibilities of a professor to teach the truth of Christianity.

In his *Treatise of Human Nature* Hume notes the 'contagiousness' described by Hutcheson. 'No quality of human nature is more remarkable,' he writes, 'both in itself and in its consequences, than that propensity we have to sympathize with others.' This sympathy is 'the soul or animating principle' of all passions, not just the joyful ones to which Hutcheson refers in the lecture quoted earlier.[11] These passions are not locked in some sort of struggle with reason; instead, reason 'is, and ought only to be the slave of the passions, and can never pretend to any other office than to service and obey them'.[12] Nor is it helpful to posit a free will that might command the passions or allow us to choose to follow reason; this will is just another 'impression'. For all the noise made about it, the idea of free will in fact has little influence on 'our vulgar and popular ways of thinking'.[13] It is 'custom' that links cause with effect and which influences our passions, more than sympathy ever could. Hume does, however, see sympathy as explaining why we admire the rich, as well as why we admire rules adopted for the 'interest of society'.[14]

Though Hume followed Hutcheson in speaking of a moral sense that allow us to perceive right and wrong, he disagreed with Hutcheson in arguing that our concept of justice is also founded on custom, not on the general goodwill (benevolence) to mankind that Hutcheson based it on. This emphasis on custom invited a more anthropological approach to the study of institutions, to 'philosophical history', the study of how moral norms change over time. The French legal scholar Montesquieu's *De l'Esprit des*

Lois (The Spirit of the Laws, 1748) had analysed law as a product, not of the will of this or that individual king or law-giver, but of the manners, climate, religion and ethos of the society concerned. So did the work of Henry Home, an Edinburgh lawyer Smith also encountered in these years, better known as Lord Kames, the title he took when he was appointed a judge in the Court of Sessions in 1752. Kames's *Essays on Several Subjects Concerning British Antiquities* (1747) adopted a stadial model of human development; that is, one that saw human society as advancing through a series of stages (such as 'feudalism', a word Montesquieu used regularly), each of them accompanied by a set of laws and customs. Kames's interests ranged widely, from legal history through natural religion to rhetoric and aesthetics. Yet he was also active in more practical endeavours, promoting the Scottish linen industry, new methods of crop rotation and other practical improvements to Scottish agriculture in his *Progress of Flax-Husbandry in Scotland* (1766) as well as *The Gentleman Farmer* (1776).

Kames was 27 years older than Smith, and took him under his wing, inviting him to prepare two series of public lectures on rhetoric and jurisprudence, which Smith delivered in Edinburgh (where exactly is not known) between 1748 and 1751. The texts of both series are lost. Some of the material on rhetoric was probably recycled in an essay on the origin of language published in 1761, while the jurisprudence series was presumably not very different from the series Smith delivered at Glasgow in 1762, for which we have student notes. In his discussion of language Smith shows that language originates in the needs of primitive man, rather than being (as was widely held at the time) a gift from God. In rhetoric Smith takes 'propriety' (appropriateness, fitness) as the best guide to eloquence, to a pure, unaffected style. Since rhetoric is about communication and above all persuasion, it follows that 'it is the custom of the people that forms what we call propriety' (*LRBL*, 5). When we boil down 'the Rules of Criticism' applicable to literature

Lord Kames (left) with the advocate Hugo Arnot and one of his fellow Edinburgh judges, Lord Monboddo, *c.* 1784.

and public speaking, therefore, we find a rule of propriety 'equally applicable to conversation and behaviour as [to] writing'. The test of propriety lies in whether we spectators 'find ourselves inclined to give our assent' or approval to the 'sentiments' expressed by the actor (*LRBL*, 55). This process by which spectators 'go along with' an actor lies at the heart of Smith's moral philosophy in *The Theory of Moral Sentiments*.

In October 1751 Smith was appointed to the chair of logic at the University of Glasgow. His 1748 lectures on rhetoric had attracted a good, paying audience of around a hundred influential people, and been enough of a success for him to repeat them in 1749 and 1750. Kames would presumably have been pleased with Smith's attention to 'the effects that derive from human nature itself, from our passions and from the natural spring of our actions' – effects Kames felt Montesquieu had not considered enough.[15] Family connections, however, also played a role in the appointment at Glasgow. Smith's former guardian, the Kirkcaldy merchant and landowner James Oswald, was now an MP, and wrote to the Duke of Argyll and fellow MPs urging them to keep 'one Mr Adam Smith' in mind for any professorships that came open, introducing him as 'Cousin to [William] Smith who was about ye late Duke', that is, who had been in service to the former Duke of Argyll.[16] In 1751 it was clear that the Glasgow chair in moral philosophy was likely to become vacant, too, as Hutcheson's successor in that post, Thomas Craigie, was ill. Hume hoped to get it, and privately Smith was delighted at the prospect of having his eminent friend as a colleague, but wrote to a friend that he was 'afraid the public would not be of my opinion; and the interest of the society [i.e. the university] will oblige us to have some regard to the opinion of the public' (c, 5).

After time spent as a private tutor and travelling across Europe as a diplomatic secretary, Hume had returned to Scotland in 1749. He had published more essays as well as *An Enquiry Concerning the Principles of Morals* (1751), a pithier version of the arguments in the *Treatise*, emphasizing utility as the basis of our moral judgments. Although Hume claimed to Hutcheson to have stripped the *Treatise* of any material likely to offend the orthodox, his failure to secure the Edinburgh chair back in 1744 had led him to be much more forthright in subsequent publications. In his *An Enquiry Concerning Human Understanding* (1748) he seemed to be arguing that most works of 'divinity or school metaphysics' were worth using only as firewood. Hume was not appointed; indeed, he never held a teaching position in any university. Instead Smith was 'translated', exchanging his chair in logic for this chair in moral philosophy.

What was Smith's view of the state of this 'science'? Although *The Theory of Moral Sentiments* was published in 1759, it is worth jumping ahead at this point to consider Part VII of that work, in which Smith outlines the different 'systems of moral philosophy' that had been developed before him, from the Stoics and Epicureans of the classical world to those advanced by Mandeville and Hutcheson. All of these systems have something to offer us, but all also contain errors, many due to a tendency Smith had already observed in his 'History of Astronomy'. This 'propensity to account for all appearances from as few principles as possible' is 'natural to all men', but philosophers are particularly prone to suffer from it, out of a vain love 'of displaying their ingenuity' (*TMS*, 299). In considering such 'systems of moral philosophy' Smith writes that we need to bear two questions in mind: 'First, wherein does virtue consist?' Some systems saw virtue as consisting in the 'government' or control of our passions (in propriety), others in the pursuit of our own interest (in prudence), still others in the selfless pursuit of the happiness of others (in benevolence). 'And, secondly, by what power or faculty in the mind is it, that this character, whatever it be, is recommended to us?'; that is, how do we come to prefer right to wrong behaviour (*TMS*, 265)? It is important to remember that in using terms such as 'right' and 'wrong' Smith is not referring to any prior, given concepts. We simply attach the word 'right' to the kind of 'praise-worthy' behaviour we approve of. We do not praise because the behaviour is good; rather, it is good because we praise it (*TMS*, 165). This approval is not a product of our free will, it arises naturally. This process is discussed in more depth in the following chapter.

Smith begins by considering 'Systems which make Virtue consist in Propriety'. He considers the ancient Greek philosopher Aristotle's notion of virtue as being a happy medium between opposing vices, or based on habits of 'moderation' (*TMS*, 271). He also considers his beloved Stoics, who held that 'every animal was by nature recommended to its own care, and was endowed with the principle of self-love' sufficient to lead it to choose whatever was conducive to its well-being (*TMS*, 272). But the Stoics understood that the self was just one individual in a vast universe, and so where necessary its well-being should yield to that of the whole. Unfortunately, the violence of the age left the leading Stoics in such insecurity that they sought consolation in sublime yet harsh indifference to life, which according to myth extended even to advocating cheerful suicide. They mistake 'sublime contemplation' for 'the great business and occupation of our lives', when nature intended it as 'the consolation of our misfortunes' (*TMS*, 292). The trouble with all these systems is that they do not answer Smith's second question: they do not provide 'any precise or distinct measure by which this fitness or propriety of affection can be ascertained or judged of' (*TMS*, 294). Smith believes that his system of sympathy provides that judge.

He then turns to prudence, and to the Epicureans, who saw virtue as anything that led to 'ease of body . . . and in security or tranquillity of mind'. Smith is surprised that despite Epicurus' reputation as a sociable man, he is ignorant of the evident fact that we desire the praise of others more than we do our own ease and pleasure: 'that to be amiable, to be respectable, to be the proper object of esteem, is by every well-disposed mind more valued than all the ease and security which love, respect, and esteem can procure us' (*TMS*, 298). Unless and until we enjoy the esteem or affection of others, it is hard for us to find 'ease' in anything else. Epicurus also erred in seeing virtue as having no appeal to us other than as a means to happiness: whereas Smith held that this was reinforced by an aesthetic admiration for 'the natural beauty of virtue' (*TMS*, 296 and 299).

Smith then turns to consider those systems which made virtue consist in benevolence. Among these it is Hutcheson's which comes in for highest praise: 'the most acute, the most distinct, the most philosophical, and what is of the most greatest consequence of all, the soberest and most judicious' (*TMS*, 301). Though this system is likely to encourage the highest virtues, it is too harsh when it claims that 'Self-love was a principle which could never be virtuous in any degree or in any direction', and sees 'self-approbation' as 'a selfish motive' (*TMS*, 303). 'Regard to our own private happiness and interest . . . appear upon many occasions very laudable principles of action', Smith counters, and 'self-interested motives' lead us to develop several 'very praise-worthy qualities' and habits: frugality, hard work, discretion and thoughtful planning (*TMS*, 304). As the

Stoics note, we have a duty of self-preservation. A man who does not 'take that proper care of his health, his life, or his fortune' would, Smith notes, be 'universally disapproved of' – and *not* on the ground that it showed a lack of benevolence.

It would be unfair to expect fallible, weak humans to pursue pure benevolence and disapprove of any mixture of it with a concern for one's 'self-preservation':

> Benevolence may, perhaps, be the sole principle of action in the Deity, and there are several, not improbable, arguments which tend to persuade us that it is so. It is not easy to conceive what other motive an independent and all-perfect Being, who stands in need of nothing external, and whose happiness is complete in himself, can act from. But whatever may be the case with the Deity, so imperfect a creature as man, the support of whose existence requires so many things external to him, must often act from many other motives. The condition of human nature [would be] peculiarly hard, if those affections, which, by the very nature of our being, ought frequently to influence our conduct, could upon no occasion appear virtuous, or deserve esteem and commendation from any body (*TMS*, 305).

As for Hutcheson's 'moral sense', which led us to perceive right and wrong, it was absurd. Our other, familiar senses were not directed at just two qualities, as Hutcheson's sense was supposed to be. After all, 'Who ever thought of calling the sense of seeing black or white, the sense of hearing loud or low, or the sense of tasting sweet or bitter?' (*TMS*, 323).

Though Smith discusses Mandeville under the heading of 'licentious' systems, in a way Smith's critique of Mandeville is similar to his critique of Hutcheson. While Hutcheson blamed any action that was not motivated by universal benevolence, Smith wrote that:

It is the great fallacy of Dr Mandeville's book to represent every passion as wholly vicious, which is so in any degree and in any direction. It is thus that he treats every thing as vanity which has any reference, either to what are, or to what ought to be the sentiments of others: and it is by means of this sophistry, that he establishes his favourite conclusion, that private vices are public benefits (*TMS*, 312–13).

Mandeville was also guilty of overlooking the distinction between praise and praiseworthiness, and associating both with vanity. Smith acknowledges that individuals often act from a combination, that the two are 'blended together', but argues that it is foolish to follow Mandeville in attributing 'to the love of praise . . . every action which ought to be ascribed to that of praise-worthiness' (*TMS*, 126–7). 'The desire of doing what is honourable and noble, of rendering ourselves the proper objects of esteem and approbation, cannot with any propriety be called vanity' (*TMS*, 309). We all condemn those who seek praise without being praiseworthy (as we cannot sympathize with them). We are led to do so by the judge we derive from Smith's model of sympathy, who is always checking that any praise is merited. This sympathy and this judge are fully explained in the earlier parts of *The Theory of Moral Sentiments*, to which we turn in the next chapter.

2

Spectatorship and Sympathy, 1751–63

In 1751 Smith returned to Glasgow, where he filled the chair in
moral philosophy that had been Hutcheson's. Smith's inaugural
lecture (now lost) was delivered in Latin and entitled *De origine
idearum* (On the Origin of Ideas). Thanks to the reforms carried
out under Hutcheson, Smith could deliver the rest of his lectures in
English, although he was still expected to begin each lecture with
a prayer, a duty he apparently performed somewhat grudgingly.[1]
Like Hutcheson, Smith took an interest in the university's
administration, overseeing its finances as 'Quaestor' and serving
as Dean and Rector. He was thus in a position to ensure that the
university library bought the first seven volumes of the famous
French *Encyclopédie* edited by Denis Diderot and Jean le Rond
d'Alembert, a monument of the European Enlightenment whose
entry for 'Pin' featured an engraved illustration of the famous
pin factory. In 1759 Smith's *The Theory of Moral Sentiments* was
published. It brought Smith to the attention of the leading thinkers
of the Enlightenment, particularly after it was translated into French
(1764) and German (1768). 'We have nothing to compare with him,'
wrote the French philosopher Voltaire, 'and I am embarrassed
for my dear compatriots.' 'Where in Germany,' wondered Kant,
'is the man who can write so well about the moral character?'[2]
Clearly these men of the Enlightenment were not above expressing
a patriotic concern for how their national 'team' was faring in the
philosophy stakes.

The Pope was less impressed, and *The Theory of Moral Sentiments* was placed on the Index Librorum Prohibitorum, the list of heretical or immoral books that Roman Catholics were forbidden to read, and which was regularly updated between 1559 and 1966. Smith probably took it as a compliment to join the likes of Kepler, Hume, Diderot, Voltaire and Kant (although Kant was put on the list only later). A copy of *The Theory of Moral Sentiments* cost six shillings, and the edition of around a thousand copies did rather better than Hume's *Treatise of Human Nature* had. Further editions followed. Students came from Switzerland and Russia to study under Smith at Glasgow. Smith's income as professor came partly from student fees (one and a half guineas per course) and partly direct from the university. He supplemented this income by acting as the private tutor to Thomas Fitzmaurice, the younger son of John Petty, 1st Earl of Shelburne. Thomas moved into Smith's house and lived under his constant supervision. Smith oversaw his allowance and moral education as well as having him attend university lectures and read Montesquieu. Other members of the Smith household were Smith's cousin Jane Douglas (who acted as housekeeper) and Smith's beloved mother Margaret. Though the city's cultural life lagged behind Edinburgh, in the early 1750s Smith joined and in some cases helped establish a series of new clubs and institutions devoted to political economy, philosophy and the 'polite arts' of painting and sculpture.

Smith delivered his lectures at the painfully early hour of 7:30 am, spending the rest of the day in tutorials, during which he led small groups of students in conversations intended to reinforce and further illustrate the material covered in that morning's lecture. Students thus got to see Smith as the performer behind the lectern and to observe his more 'private' character. 'His private character is really amiable,' James Boswell (a student) noted, 'he has none of that formal stiffness and Pedantry which is too often found in Professors.'[3] Students clearly came to view Professor Smith

William Hogarth, *The Laughing Audience*, 1735, engraving: even if we can't see the play, we still smile.

as something of a local celebrity: his portrait bust was sold in shops near the university grounds.[4]

A colleague, John Millar, later recalled Smith's moral philosophy syllabus:

His course of lectures on this subject was divided into four parts. The first contained Natural Theology; in which he considered the proofs of the being and attributes of God, and those principles of the human mind upon which religion is founded. The second comprehended Ethics, strictly so called, and consisted chiefly of the doctrines which he afterwards published in his Theory of Moral Sentiments. In the third part, he treated at more length of that branch of morality which relates to *justice*, and which, being susceptible of precise and accurate rules, is for that reason capable of a full and particular explanation.

Upon this subject he followed the plan that seems to be suggested by Montesquieu; endeavouring to trace the gradual progress of jurisprudence, both public and private, from the rudest to the most refined ages, and to point out the effects of those arts which contribute to subsistence, and to the accumulation of property, in producing corresponding improvements or alterations in law and government . . .

In the last part of his lecture, he examined those political regulations which are founded, not upon the principle of *justice*, but that of *expediency*, and which are calculated to increase the riches, the power, and the prosperity of a State.[5]

Though the first and third parts are entirely lost, the fourth was turned into *The Wealth of Nations*. It is the second part, however, that concerns us here.

The system of moral philosophy advanced in *The Theory of Moral Sentiments* is founded on sympathy – the 'contagiousness' that Hutcheson had noted and which Hume had considered, but not seen as being of central importance. Smith opens Part I of *The Theory of Moral Sentiments* by explaining how it works. Today sympathy is often understood as a kind of sentiment or emotion in itself, as a kind of humanitarian sorrow expressed in response to the suffering of others. 'Have you no pity?' and 'Have you no sympathy?' are seemingly interchangeable. As such it is often linked to benevolence, even if we usually speak of sympathy *for* the unhappy, rather than sympathy *with* the happy. For Smith, sympathy is not a feeling or sentiment but the means by which we become aware of any and all sentiments. We do not *feel* Smith's sympathy *for* someone else. We *have* or *experience* all kinds of passions by means of sympathy, which Smith insists we use 'to denote our fellow-feeling with any passion whatever' (*TMS*, 10). The word 'empathy' did not exist in Smith's day, but there are cases in which the reader may find it more helpful to use that term. It is less common, for example, to confuse 'empathy' with a feeling; 'empathy' also tends to be preferred by philosophers and scientists. Here however, we shall use Smith's term.

Smith sees sympathy as automatic in everyone. One did not have to live the life of a Stoic, a life of 'sublime contemplation', to acquire it. On the contrary, even criminals have it:

> How selfish soever man may be supposed, there are evidently some principles in his nature, which interest him in the fortune of others, and render their happiness necessary to him, though he derives nothing from it except the pleasure of seeing it. Of this kind is pity or compassion, the emotion which we feel for the misery of others, when we either see it, or are made to conceive it in a very lively manner. That we often derive sorrow from the sorrow of others, is a matter of fact too obvious to require any instances to prove it; for this sentiment, like all the other original passions of human nature, is by no means confined to the virtuous and humane, though they perhaps may feel it with the most exquisite sensibility. The greatest ruffian, the most hardened violator of the laws of society, is not altogether without it (*TMS*, 9).

We should not consider sympathy to be a rare quality; Smith says that everybody is capable of 'fellow-feeling' without giving it any thought at all.

For Smith sympathy does not mean feeling what the other person is feeling, but what we ourselves would feel, were we

The final scene of Hogarth's *A Rake's Progress* (1735) shows the rake in Bedlam, where genteel visitors like the lady with the fan came to give themselves a sentimental workout.

placed in their situation. If we felt exactly what the other person felt, sympathy would no longer fulfil the important purpose Smith assigns to it, that is, the regulation of the passions: the achievement of that virtuous 'moderation' that Aristotle had placed somewhere between the vices associated with too much and too little passion. Sympathy helps 'tune' the passions to a level that holds a community together rather than tearing it apart. Smith illustrates this by reference to our ability to sympathize with the dead and with the insane. Although the dead individual no longer feels or can feel any passion, we nonetheless transpose ourselves into their state of 'being dead' and imagine living (as it were) without being able to feel anything. We find that horrifying. This, Smith concludes, is why we fear death. This fear is one reason Smith found stories of Stoics cheerfully killing themselves 'marvellous', in the sense of unbelievable (*TMS*, 285).

Visiting insane asylums such as London's Bethlem Royal Hospital (known as Bedlam) was something of a 'polite' pastime in Adam Smith's day, with hospitals even encouraging visits by the gentry as a means of raising contributions from the benevolent. Although they were probably just a manifestation of the time-honoured love of a good gawp, such visits were often justified as an opportunity for the visitors to display their 'sensibility': to prove to each other how feeling (or 'sensible' – that is, capable of feeling sentiments) they were, by giving their passions (and tear ducts) a good workout. The hero of Henry Mackenzie's popular novel *The Man of Feeling* (1771) visits Bedlam, where he weeps profusely. Smith has little time for such fashionable antics by 'whining and melancholy moralists'. Like Aristotle, for Smith virtue was about action, not feeling; beneficence (doing good), not benevolence (wishing good) (*TMS*, 139). He does however see our sorrowful response to an apparently happy psychotic person as instructive:

> The poor wretch, who is [insane], laughs and sings perhaps, and is altogether insensible of his own misery. The anguish which humanity feels, therefore, at the sight of such an object, cannot be the reflection of any sentiment of the sufferer. The compassion of the spectator must arise altogether from the consideration of what he himself would feel if he was reduced to the same unhappy situation, and, what perhaps is impossible, was at the same time able to regard it with his present reason and judgment (*TMS*, 12).

In the case of the insane, therefore, we do not sympathize with a passion that we think unjustified by the circumstances. We put ourselves in the insane man's situation, not his mind. He feels happy, we are sad.

Having considered how we judge others, Smith considers how we judge our own conduct. Smith believes that we seek to approve of ourselves, and that the love of such 'self-approbation' is the love of virtue (*TMS*, 117). As we have seen, this was very different from Hutcheson's and Mandeville's view. Again Smith makes a distinction between 'praise' and 'praiseworthiness'. It is one thing, he says, to receive approval from others; another to know that we deserve such praise. Part of us craves the praise of others and seeks to avoid their censure. Smith calls this 'the man without', and claims that only the 'weak, the vain and the frivolous' are fully satisfied with how things appear on the surface, before that 'inferiour tribunal' (*TMS*, 130). This is because all of us learn as children that praise and blame are often given to those who do not deserve it, owing to the natural messiness of the world as it is (*TMS*, 62).

Thus we put ourselves in front of a 'higher tribunal', a higher court, whose judge looks beyond appearances to consider whether we earned that praise or that blame, whether we are in fact praise- or blame-worthy: 'We . . . sett up in our own minds a judge between ourselves and those we live with . . . a person quite candid and equitable, . . . who has no particular relation either to ourselves, or to those whose interests are affected by our conduct' (*TMS*, 129). This will often involve considering the motivations that lie behind an action, rather than the action alone. Smith calls this judge 'the man within the breast' or the 'impartial spectator'. This judge is always with us, even when we are alone, and his judgements affect us more deeply than those of the 'inferiour tribunal'. Smith sometimes refers to this judge as a kind of deity, a 'Demigod', poised halfway between the court of our peers and the 'still higher tribunal' of God, who places 'a degree of obscurity and darkness' between his judgements and ours (*TMS*, 131 and 129). Whereas God is omniscient and feels only benevolence, this 'impartial spectator' has human limitations and human potential. Though well-informed, this spectator cannot know everything; though the 'spectator's' passions may appear muted by 'self-command', unlike God the spectator has the full gamut of human emotion. The Impartial Spectator, therefore, is more than a kind of halfway house, more than a 'Goldilocks' spectator (that is, one neither too passionately 'hot' nor Stoically 'cold'). On the contrary, this spectator displays a mastery of which God is incapable.

The discovery in the 1980s of mirror neurons by neuro-physiologists Giacomo Rizzolatti and Vittorio Gallese suggests that the responses Smith suggests we have to others' emotional and physical states may in a sense be hard-wired. Mirror neurons are neurons found in human brains that fire both when we perform an action as well as when we observe another animal perform the same action. Experiments using functional magnetic resonance imaging (fMRI) have found similar mirroring involving displays of emotions like happiness, pain and disgust. Areas of the brain that fire when we feel disgust have been observed also to fire when we see a face wearing an expression of disgust.[6] Such research is ongoing, and its possible implications are far from clear. By all accounts the human brain is 'plastic'; that is, it can in a sense rewire itself in response to the demands placed on it. Even if there is some sort of relationship between mirror neurons and the sympathetic human culture described by Smith, it may not be causal, and, even if causal, the causality may not run the way we might expect. In so far as mirror neurons are also found in the brains of our fellow primates, it may force us to revisit Smith's sharp distinction between humans and all other animals. Smith holds that the universe is intended to serve one purpose: human society. Whereas Hume claimed that humans can sympathize with other species, Smith never considers the possibility.[7] His world view is unrepentantly anthropocentric.

Now that we understand the mechanism behind our emotions we can look at how Smith presents the full range of human passions in the remaining part of section 1 of *The Theory of Moral Sentiments*. Compared to the way Hume organized them in *A Treatise of Human*

Mirror carved by Sefferin Alken to a design by Robert Adam (who, like Smith, was from Kirkcaldy), 1765. Look in the mirror: what do you see?

Nature, Smith's approach is easy to follow. Hume divided the passions into the productive passions (which 'produce' impressions of pleasure and pain, such as hunger and sexual appetite), the responsive passions (responses to pleasure and pain), indirect passions (pride, hatred) and compound passions (benevolence, for example). What we feel is often the result of several different passions that interact in complex ways, modified by a series of binary oppositions and principles of association linking them.

Smith divides our emotions into four groups: 'the passions which take their origin from the body', the 'unsocial passions', the 'social passions' and the 'selfish passions'. He then considers each passion in isolation, something Hume finds difficult. We might expect Smith to present the social passions as good and the selfish and unsocial passions as bad; to speak of absolutes, of virtues and vices. Vice is bad because it's bad, because we just know (we intuit) that it is so. As noted in the previous chapter, however, Smith does not believe we have a Hutchesonian 'moral sense' with which to perceive right and wrong. He distinguishes passions not according to whether they are good or bad in themselves, but by the degree to which an Impartial Spectator can sympathize with them.

Let us begin our tour of the passions where Smith himself starts, with 'the passions which take their origin from the body' (*TMS*, 27). These include hunger and lust. All strong expressions of these are 'loathsome and disagreeable'. This is not because they are 'low' or brutish, but because 'when we see them in other men . . . we cannot enter into them', that is, we cannot sympathize with them. As Smith notes, reading a tragedy makes us feel sad, but reading about people starving does not make us feel hungry. The sheer amount of pornography available might lead us to question whether Smith is right about lust not being transferable in a similar manner. We might argue that this is a case in which our identification with the individual enjoying intercourse on the page or on-screen is complete: we actually become them in our imagination, and lose awareness of our ambivalent position – of the fact that we have our feet in that person's shoes (metaphorically speaking; in practice they are unlikely to be wearing any) and in our own.

If we were to give the individual the features of someone we know socially, this would no longer be possible, which may explain why watching a friend have sex would indeed be 'loathsome and disagreeable'. Another fact Smith cites in support of his argument about bodily passions is the fact that once these passions are

William Hogarth, *After*, etching and engraving, 1736.

satisfied, the object that excites that passion 'ceases to be agreeable:
even its presence becomes offensive'. This is why, Smith claims,
we clear the remains off our tables after eating; we would do the
same with our sexual partner, he argues, 'if they were objects
of no other passions but those which take their origin from the
body' (TMS, 28). In other words, if we were not drawn to our sexual
partner by other sentiments, we would immediately try to escape

their presence once we were satisfied. The man in William Hogarth's *After* certainly seems to avoid the embrace of the tearful woman who clutches him, although minutes earlier (in *Before*) she was struggling to fend him off.

Physical pain also elicits little sympathy, which is why we tone down our expression of it. Smith would have it that we do not sympathize nearly so much with the prisoner's pain while that prisoner is being tortured by someone else as we do with the fear and uncertainty they experience in between bouts of torture, caused by their imagining worse tortures to come. In a way, we sympathize with them when they are thus torturing themselves. Whereas pain is of short duration and quickly forgotten afterwards, an insult from a friend is very different: 'The agony which this creates is by no means over with the word . . . the imagination continues to fret and rankle within, from the thought of it' (*TMS*, 29). Though striking, this is surely an observation that we can all recognize as true. Can anyone remember the pain of falling and breaking an arm five years on? Yet we can recall an argument with a former lover in detail that is excruciating, and which, once recalled, is far harder to forget again.

Though it derives from the imagination rather than from the body, love is another passion Smith holds to be difficult for a spectator to sympathize with. Though we can share in a lover's distress and fear that her love may not be returned by the object of her affections, we otherwise laugh at expressions of love, and those who do feel it make a point of talking about their passion 'with raillery and ridicule'. Smith puts it pithily: 'Though a lover may be good company to his mistress, he is so to nobody else' (*TMS*, 31). This may seem dismissive, and we may wish to recall at this point that Smith himself does not seem to have had any long-term partner. It is odd that we should be able to sympathize more easily with a dead person than with someone alive, but who happens to be in love.

The 'social passions' are those that the Impartial Spectator can easily enter into: 'generosity, humanity, kindness, compassion, mutual friendship and esteem'. They are doubled, in a sense, in that 'we enter into the satisfaction both of the person who feels them, and of the person who is the object of them' (*TMS*, 38–9). Though today we tend to think of 'society' and the family as inhabiting distinct realms of public and private, Smith's most moving account of the social passions at work describes a family with two parents and multiple children:

> With what pleasure do we look upon a family, through the whole of which reign mutual love and esteem, where the parents and children are companions for one another, without any other difference than what is made by respectful attention on the one side, and kind indulgence on the other; where freedom and fondness, mutual raillery and mutual kindness, show that no opposition of interest divides the brothers, nor any rivalship of favour sets the sisters at variance, and where every thing presents us with the idea of peace, cheerfulness, harmony and contentment?

Though in one sense a sketch of intimate relations, it is far from shut off from the outside world, for 'their mutual regard renders them happy in one another, and sympathy, with this mutual regard, makes them agreeable to every other person' (*TMS*, 39). Happy families make happy societies.

The 'unsocial passions' are passions that are difficult for us to sympathize with. They include anger, spite, ingratitude and hatred. Under normal circumstances we restrain such passions because we know they can never be shared unless we tone them right down. Finally, we come to the passions that occupied Smith most, and which continue to dominate discussion of capitalism and the invisible hand: the 'selfish passions'. How does Smith see them fitting in between the other two groups?

> Besides those two opposite sets of passions, the social and unsocial, there is another which holds a sort of middle place between them; is never either so graceful as is sometimes the one set [social], nor is ever so odious as is sometimes the other [unsocial]. Grief and joy, when conceived upon account of our own private good or bad fortune, constitute this third set of passions.

Because these passions are directed towards ourselves, they can never seem 'good' or 'bad' in quite the way the passions directed towards others can be, for in the latter case there is a 'double sympathy' – that is, we can sympathize with both the actor and the beneficiary (or victim).

There is only a single sympathy in the case of an individual's 'selfish' joys and griefs, and Smith says that they do not move us equally. 'The man who, by some sudden revolution of fortune, is lifted up all at once into a condition of life, greatly above what he had formerly lived in,' he notes, 'may be assured that the congratulations of his best friends are not all of them perfectly sincere' (*TMS*, 40–41). We do not, therefore, expect much sympathy for either small sorrows or great joys. If your sorrow consists only of being 'hen-pecked by your wife', the best you can hope for from your friends is to be laughed at. A certain 'malice in mankind' finds 'little uneasinesses' amusing, which explains that 'delight which we all take in raillery, and in the small vexation which we observe in our companion, when he is pushed, and urged, and teased upon all sides'. When it comes to great sorrows, however, we can expect far more from our friends. 'We weep even at the feigned representation of a tragedy,' Smith (a keen theatregoer) notes (*TMS*, 43, 42). It is a striking instance of the comprehensiveness of Smith's moral philosophy that he explains why we enjoy both the highest tragedy as well as comedy of the commonest, most familiar 'take my wife' variety.

Like small sorrows, great joys also elicit little sympathy. By 'revolution of fortune' Smith probably means something like a sudden promotion to a high-profile position of some kind, a position that may, of course, bring a monetary windfall in the shape of a high salary. Smith says that we already recognize that others will find it difficult to sympathize with our joy at such a promotion, and so we tone our expressions of joy right down – even with our 'best friends'. We show the full measure of joy we feel only to those very close to us, such as our parents and partners. As Smith says, 'What is called affection, is in reality nothing but habitual sympathy', and our parents and partners are the most practised at sympathizing with us, and hence the best at going along with our passions (*TMS*, 220).

It is our longing to share our passions that makes us prefer a more measured progress to that high rank or position. Sudden wealth does not, therefore, bring happiness:

> If the chief part of human happiness arises from the consciousness of being beloved, as I believe it does, those sudden changes of fortune seldom contribute much to happiness. He is happiest who advances more gradually to greatness, whom the public destines to every step of his preferment long before he arrives at it, in whom, upon that account, when it comes, it can excite no extravagant joy, and with regard to whom it cannot reasonably create either any jealousy in those he overtakes, or any envy in those he leaves behind (*TMS*, 41).

The reference to his own belief is striking here. Smith tends to use a rather clunky phrase ('if I may say so' or, more commonly, 'if I may so say') just before introducing a dramatic image or analogy, asking the reader's leave as if about to use some indelicate or unphilosophical expression. But for him to go further and use the phrase 'as I believe it does' is unusually assertive. The surrounding account of the alienating effect of sudden wealth is clearly founded on deep conviction. Because others cannot share in the joy it brings to the beneficiary, sudden wealth sets her adrift from her friends. She cannot convincingly carry off the demanding role of humility long enough to keep them, yet resentment at an upstart prevents her from finding replacements among those already wealthy. She has a foot in both camps, but is at home in neither. She enjoys no tranquillity.

Smith's debt to the Stoics is clearest in the value he sets on this tranquillity, on *ataraxia*. As we noted in the previous chapter, Smith felt that the Stoics had become carried away and begun arguing that 'sublime contemplation' or cheerful suicide were the noblest ends of life precisely because the times they were living through were so politically unstable that tranquillity could be enjoyed only in death, or squatting in Diogenes' barrel. Fortunately for us, living in the relatively peaceful 'Age of Commerce', tranquillity is within our reach:

> Happiness consists in tranquillity and enjoyment. Without tranquillity there can be no enjoyment; and where there is perfect tranquillity there is scarce any thing which is not capable of amusing. But in every permanent situation, where there is no expectation of change, the mind of every man, in a longer or shorter time, returns to its natural and usual state of tranquillity. In prosperity, after a certain time, it falls back to that state; in adversity, after a certain time, it rises up to it ... The great source of both the misery and disorders of human life, seems to arise from over-rating the difference between one permanent situation and another. Avarice over-rates the difference between poverty and riches: ambition, that between a private and a public station: vain-glory, that between obscurity and extensive reputation.

Smith argues that along with sympathy, which allows us to achieve the tranquillity that comes with always enjoying the right level of passion, nature has also endowed us with a destabilizing and anxiety-inducing love of 'bettering our condition'. If the harmful effects were limited to the ambitious individual, that would be bad enough. Unfortunately, the person under the influence of avarice, ambition and vainglory is not only 'miserable in his actual situation, but is often disposed to disturb the peace of society', by violating 'the rules either of prudence or of justice' (*TMS*, 149).

There is something curious about this ambition to 'better our condition'. In the parable of the Poor Man's Son quoted in the Introduction it is paradoxical that the anti-hero is driven to expend years of punishing effort struggling to become rich because he thinks he is lazy ('indolent') and wants to be waited on hand and foot. A man who is actually lazy would never bother working as hard as the Poor Man's Son does. Far from being indolent, the Poor Man's Son is a very busy man, in the pejorative sense that 'busy' had in the eighteenth century: careworn and constantly fussing, usually with things of no importance. This 'busyness' is something Smith smiles at, in the same way we might wonder at a child whose entire attention is taken up with a 'busy box' of toys. As we shall see, 'toys' nonetheless play a far from trifling role in Smith's vision of human history.

A note of wonder at the delusions of the 'bustler in business' is always there (*TMS*, 215):

> For to what purpose is all the toil and bustle of this world? What is the end of avarice and ambition, of the pursuit of wealth, of power, and preheminence? Is it to supply the necessities of nature? The wages of the meanest labourer can supply them. We see that they afford him food and clothing, the comfort of a house, and of a family. If we examined his oeconomy with rigour, we should find that he spends a great part of them upon

conveniencies, which may be regarded as superfluities, and that, upon extraordinary occasions, he can give something even to vanity and distinction.

This may seem fanciful at first glance, but the consistent upwards movement of supposedly fixed 'poverty lines' as well as the very different points at which they have been and are drawn today surely suggests that we should not dismiss this out of hand. Why is a television set considered a 'luxury' in one part of the world, and a 'conveniency' or even a 'necessity' in others?

We don't want money or power in order to provide for our needs. We know, Smith insists, that the rich man does not enjoy better digestion or sounder sleep as a result of having fine food and a large house. Indeed, 'the contrary has been so often observed, and, indeed, is so very obvious, though it had never been observed, that there is nobody ignorant of it.' (*TMS*, 50) Elsewhere Smith urges his readers to consider rich people whom they know, rather than simply taking his word for it. And we would urge the reader to do the same, while pointing to scientific studies of statistically significant samples of people that suggest Smith is right: the Easterlin Paradox, for example, is widely recognized.

We seek money and power because we wish to have attention paid to us – to 'be attended to', in Smith's parlance:

To be observed, to be attended to, to be taken notice of with sympathy, complacency, and approbation, are all the advantages which we can propose to derive from it. It is the vanity, not the ease, or the pleasure, which interests us. But vanity is always founded upon the belief of our being the object of attention and approbation. The rich man glories in his riches, because he feels that they naturally draw upon him the attention of the world, and that mankind are disposed to go along with him in all those agreeable emotions with which the advantages of his situation

A father almost fails to recognize his fashionable son, who is literally making a spectacle of himself in this mezzotint by Carington Bowles after Samuel Hieronymus, *Grimm, Welladay! Is this My Son Tom!*, 1774.

so readily inspire him. At the thought of this, his heart seems to swell and dilate itself within him, and he is fonder of his wealth, upon this account, than for all the other advantages it procures him (*TMS*, 50–51).

'The attention of the world', however, imposes a 'restraint' and a 'loss of liberty' on the rich (*TMS*, 51). Not only do they lose privacy, they lose freedom of movement. Again, one need only think of the constrained lifestyles of today's actors, royalty and heads of state to acknowledge this to be correct.

It is important to note that Smith here speaks of the rich man as an 'object of observation' and 'interest' as much as of 'fellow-feeling'. Moral approval or disapproval does not seem to be involved, perhaps because the observers here are not the rich man's friends, but strangers. 'Public admiration' of the 'great' is, Smith says, acquired without much effort, cheaply or at an 'easy price' (*TMS*, 53). The rich seem to inhabit a higher and happier plane of existence, and we consider ourselves privileged if we can, in however small a way, contribute to that happiness. The rich set the fashions that we follow, in clothing, in the way we speak and even in the way we behave, to the extent that their bad behaviour can seem worthy of emulation. Indeed, Smith calls our near veneration of the 'rich and powerful' the 'universal cause' of the corruption of our moral sentiments, because it leads us to admire 'wealth and greatness' rather than 'wisdom and virtue'. Yet this 'universal cause' is, for all Smith's discomfort at stating so, 'natural', and hence above criticism (*TMS*, 61–2).

This account of human behaviour seems odd to us, because this envy is entirely without resentment or jealousy. Nor is our attentiveness motivated by a desire for handouts or some other favour. Far from feeling that their state of apparent bliss is undeserved or wishing to see them fall, we take vicarious pleasure in observing their lifestyle and respond sympathetically to even the slightest blip in their fortunes without feeling any *Schadenfreude*. At first this seems difficult to believe, but if we think of the cult of celebrity, Smith's points begin to make sense. Magazines such as *Hello!* and *People* do indeed pick over the smallest details of the lives of 'the great', indulging in extensive speculation over the state of their personal relationships and expressing deep sorrow when they or their families are struck by illness. Aliens visiting our planet would be forced to some odd and uncomfortable (for us) conclusions. Or, as Smith puts it,

> A stranger to human nature, who saw the indifference
> of men about the misery of their inferiors, and the regret
> and indignation which they feel for the misfortunes and
> sufferings of those above them, would be apt to imagine,
> that pain must be more agonizing, and the convulsions
> of death more terrible to persons of higher rank, than to
> those of meaner stations (*TMS*, 52).

Smith tries to limit the potential damage by arguing that most of us 'in the inferior and middling stations of life' are not in a position to ape the behaviour of the great (*TMS*, 63). Our success in the lower stations depends too much on keeping in with our neighbours by regular habits, and that is just as well. This nonetheless does not seem fully to address the risks of having our moral judgements perverted as a result of our endeavouring to ape the 'manners and customs of the great'. In this regard Smith may simply be too much of his time – a time before the existence of that celebrity culture that is so effective at spoiling our tranquillity, with its promise of a kind of fame that in Smith's day was enjoyed only by kings (who owed it entirely to accident of birth).

Sympathy thus gives us a mechanism for achieving the appropriate level of every sort of passion, one founded on the innate interest we all take in each other's welfare, and constantly reinforcing that concern. It is doubtless beneficial to us as individuals and to society as a whole that this sympathy commonly leads us to lower the level of passion we might otherwise express. But is Smith suggesting that we must learn to mask our true passions behind an 'assumed appearance', that sympathy leads us to pretend that we feel less strongly than we in fact do? No, he insists that sharing our passions 'will really compose us' (*TMS*, 23). Smith is using 'compose' here in the sense of 'to calm, pacify, tranquillize'.[8] Rather than being a mask we put on reluctantly, in sorrow at the fact that others cannot feel the same degree of passion as we feel, we carry out this act of 'composition' eagerly, because we long for the pleasurable release and relief that comes when others sympathize with us.

'The person principally concerned' is aware of the fact that others can never feel with 'the same degree of violence' and at the same time 'passionately desires a more complete sympathy. He longs for that relief' (*TMS*, 22). Sharing our (somewhat flattened) passions with others is a source of pleasure in itself, even when the passion shared is unpleasant, such as grief (*TMS*, 15). In experiments where two female friends viewed a series of photographs of 'emotionally positive' situations (toddlers embracing) as well as emotionally 'neutral' and 'negative' situations, the 'social sharing of emotions' has been demonstrated to stimulate what neuroscientists call 'the reward circuitry' in the brain. This circuitry activated strongly when the images were accompanied with a display text informing the friends that they were viewing the pictures at the same time – much more so than when the images came after a text informing them that they were watching them alone. Regardless of whether the images were emotionally 'positive' or 'negative', sharing with a friend felt good – even though that friend was out of sight in another room, lying down inside an fMRI scanner.[9]

This is not a betrayal of a 'true self' because it is nearly impossible to imagine a member of a social species like *Homo sapiens* living alone. Even if 'a human creature could grow up to manhood in some solitary place, without any communication with his own species', without the 'mirror' offered by others he would not even be able to conceive of himself having passions. All he would be about to think about would be 'external objects' (*TMS*, 110). Sympathy doesn't just 'compose' us in the sense of calming our passions, it also 'composes' us in the sense that it 'constitutes' or 'constructs' our self, our 'I'.[10] Is it possible, we might well ask, for this self to experience any passion that cannot be shared with others, or with that stand-in for others, the Impartial Spectator?

Our judgement of the propriety of any display of passion, Smith says, relates the passion back to the cause that elicited that passion. In Part II of *The Theory of Moral Sentiments*, however, Smith turns to 'another set of qualities ascribed to the actions and conduct of mankind', which relates the passion to 'the beneficial or hurtfull effects which the affection [i.e. passion] proposes or tends to produce' – working forwards rather than backwards. This is our sense not of propriety and impropriety, but of merit and demerit, reward and punishment (*TMS*, 67). Once again sympathy is the mechanism, although the picture is more complicated as we are usually confronted with at least two parties: the person who acts and the person who is acted upon – the person who is benefited or harmed by the person acting. To what extent can we, the spectator, sympathize with the motives of the person acting and the response of the person acted upon? Actions with merit, 'actions of a beneficent tendency' that deserve reward, are simply those where the recipient's gratitude is appropriate, those actions that 'excite the sympathetic gratitude of the spectator' – that is, us, the observers who are not directly involved (*TMS*, 78).

Smith can now develop notions of 'beneficence' and 'justice', which he relates to merit and demerit respectively. Beneficence is 'free', as we do not enforce gratitude. Ingratitude may disappoint us and provoke our 'hatred' of the ungrateful person, but 'it cannot, however, provoke any resentment which mankind will go along with.' The distinction between 'hatred' and 'resentment' is significant: the latter leads us to punish, and is elicited only 'by actions which tend to do real and positive hurt to some particular persons'. Justice is founded on this resentment, which, Smith says, 'seems to have been given us by nature for defence, and for defence only. It is the safeguard of justice and the security of innocence' (*TMS*, 78–9). Justice does not, therefore, lead us to enforce beneficence.

Resentment offers another example where the action of sympathy can lead us to express a different degree and even a different kind of passion than that of the person we are observing. Smith asks us to imagine what we feel when we watch someone tamely accepting a barrage of insults. A Stoic or a Christian would say that we praise the victim; either because this person is dismissing pain as just another attempt to rob them of their *ataraxia*, or because this person is 'turning the other cheek' and apparently forgiving the tormentor. With his focus on benevolence, Hutcheson would say that we feel sorrow for the poor victim, and blame the tormentor. Is this what in fact happens?

A person becomes contemptible who tamely sits still, and submits to insults, without attempting either to repel or to revenge them. We cannot enter into his indifference and insensibility: we call his behaviour mean-spiritedness, and are as really provoked by it as by the insolence of his adversary. Even the mob are enraged to see any man submit patiently to affronts and ill-usage. They desire to see this insolence resented, and resented by the person who suffers from it. They cry to him with fury, to defend, or to revenge himself. If his indignation rouses at last, they heartily applaud, and sympathize with it. It enlivens their own indignation against his enemy, whom they rejoice to see him attack in his turn, and are as really gratified by his revenge, provided it is not immoderate, as if the injury had been done to themselves (*TMS*, 34–5).

As with the case of the insane man and the dead man, sympathy in fact leads us to supply, as it were, the 'missing' passion (sadness in those cases, indignation in this). But we also, Smith notes, blame the victim for being 'insensible' in a way that we do not blame the dead or insane man. We feel angry with the victim, not sorry for him. Contrary to Hutcheson, we clearly view 'self-preservation' as a praiseworthy motive. The person here is blamed because he is not taking care of himself, as everyone ought.

To Hutcheson and other contemporaries of Smith, and to many ethicists today, justice seems to come 'late' in *The Theory of Moral Sentiments*. We, too, may feel that we should start with justice and work from there. Justice should lead us to sympathy, not sympathy to justice. The justice and beneficence we reach by means of Smith's sympathy can seem limited, and limiting. Yet Smith makes it clear that our desire for justice in the above case does not result from a concern for the welfare of society or some equally abstract concept of utility:

> When a single man is injured, or destroyed, we demand the punishment of the wrong that has been done to him, not so much from a concern for the general interest of society, as from a concern for that very individual who has been injured.

A resentment felt on grounds of 'the welfare of society' would require us first to form a picture in our minds of 'society' and then consider what that abstract entity's feelings or interests might be.

Such a resentment is both time-consuming and difficult, requiring a good deal of intelligence. It cannot explain the immediacy and power with which all of us feel resentment: 'All men, even the most stupid and unthinking,' Smith notes, 'abhor fraud, perfidy, and injustice, and delight to see them punished. But few men have reflected upon the necessity of justice to the existence of society, how obvious soever that necessity may appear to be.' Whatever 'regard for the multitude' we may have is 'made up of the particular regards which we feel for the different individuals of which it is composed' (*TMS*, 89–90). Smith seeks to ground his moral philosophy in everyday interactions and in universal instincts shared by all humans, 'even the most stupid and unthinking'.

Whether or not it is supported by the internal structure of human brains, the sympathy at the heart of this moral philosophy is not perfect. Sympathy makes us the 'same person' with them, but only 'in some measure' (*TMS*, 9). This is because even while we place ourselves in another's shoes, we retain a 'secret consciousness' that a change of situation has in fact occurred (*TMS*, 22). An innovative thinker on musical aesthetics, Smith was fond of musical analogies. It might be helpful to think of emotions as sounds and sympathy as the air through which they travel. If you place an alarm clock in a glass jar you will be able to hear it ring, even if the sound is somewhat muffled. If you were to pump out the air and create a vacuum there would be no sound at all, though you would be able to see the bell being struck inside the jar. Smith's sympathy is like the air that allows emotions to 'sound' or 'echo'. We do not hear the emotions directly, but only in so far as they 'resound' or 'bounce back' off another person – what Hume called 'the double resound of the sympathy'.[11]

Rather than seeking to bring your passion and mind into complete unison (literally 'one sound', that is, of identical pitch), for sympathy to work we need only to be 'in tune'. An individual feeling a certain passion

longs for that relief which nothing can afford him but the entire concord of the affections of the spectators with his own . . . But he can only hope to obtain this by lowering his passion to that pitch, in which the spectators are capable of going along with him. He must flatten, if I may be allowed to say so, the sharpness of its natural tone, in order to reduce it to harmony and concord with the emotions of those who are about him. What they feel will, indeed, always be, in some respects, different from what he feels, and compassion can never be exactly the same with original sorrow . . . These two sentiments, however, may, it is evident, have such a correspondence with one another, as is sufficient for the harmony of society. Though they will never be unisons, they may be concords, and this is all that is wanted or required (*TMS*, 22).

Indeed, there is a sense in which the 'failure' to achieve unison can be viewed as a benefit. Unisons are very dull to listen to. Harmonics are the basis of music.

3

Trading Places, 1764–6

On 8 November 1763 Smith gave notice of his intention to resign from the University of Glasgow's chair of Moral Philosophy. Shortly after, he left for London, where he met the seventeen-year-old Henry Scott, the 3rd Duke of Buccleuch. In early February 1764 the pair crossed the Channel to France, where they remained until November 1766. Smith's task was to oversee the final years of Henry's education, preparing him for the responsibilities that would fall on his shoulders when he reached his majority (his twentieth birthday) in 1767. Smith had been hired by Henry's stepfather, the politician Charles Townshend. Townshend took his own responsibilities as guardian and trustee ('curator') of the boy's inheritance seriously. A sizeable chunk of the family's wealth had been squandered in England by Henry's grandfather, the 2nd Duke, who had been the kind of absentee landlord that gave the Scottish aristocracy such a poor reputation for ducking the social responsibilities that traditionally came with Scottish estates.

Young Henry had never visited Scotland, even though his family's wealth derived exclusively from vast landholdings stretching the forty miles from the Scottish border near Newcastleton, north through Teviotdale, the Ettrick Forest and Selkirk to Dalkeith, the family seat four miles south of Edinburgh. Henry's ancestors had amassed these lands during the Middle Ages, first as local warlords profiting from the region's lawlessness, then (from 1550) as royal appointees charged with bringing law and order and as beneficiaries of the decay of the monastic system that enabled them to acquire the vast lands of Melrose Abbey. As we shall see, the family's development from sheep-rustlers to feudal clan to absentee spendthrifts was a process Smith saw as characteristic of the aristocracy at large.

A professorship in Smith's day was a job for life. The job of tutoring Henry was clearly going to last only a few years. For Smith it would also involve spending some considerable time away from his mother and cousin, in a country whose language Smith never seems to have mastered. Tutors who accompanied young noblemen on their European tours were often called 'bearleaders', an insulting comparison with those whose job it was to look after the performing bears that were led on chains from one fair to another, where they performed tricks for tips. Like the bearleaders, travelling tutors were in an ambiguous position: on the one hand their job was to supervise and control their young clients (who, like a partly tamed bear, could and did go on the odd destructive rampage), while on the other hand the tutor was socially inferior and financially dependent on the same young man. Having hoped to make some money and get some writing done, Hume had found tutoring the unstable 3rd Marquess of Annandale far from rewarding. Hume was hired in 1745; the Marquess threw him out the following year.

Smith was among those who scoffed at the suggestion that sending young sprigs to the Continent on a 'Grand Tour' of France and Italy had any educational value:

> In England, it becomes every day more and more the custom to send young people to travel in foreign countries immediately upon their leaving school, and without sending them to any university. Our young people, it is said, generally return home much improved by their travels. A young man who goes abroad at seventeen or eighteen, and returns home at one and twenty, returns three or four years older than he was when he went

Arthur Pond after Pier Leone Ghezzi, *A Travelling Governour*, etching, 1737. Taking an aristocratic youth (a young bear) on his Grand Tour was not a job for the faint-hearted.

abroad; and at that age it is very difficult not to improve a good deal in three or four years. In the course of his travels, he generally acquires some knowledge of one or two foreign languages; a knowledge, however, which is seldom sufficient to enable him either to speak or write them with propriety. In other respects he commonly returns home more conceited, more unprincipled, more dissipated, and more incapable of any serious application either to study or to business, then he could well have become in so short a time, had he lived at home . . . Nothing but the discredit into which the universities are allowing themselves to fall, could ever have brought into repute so very absurd a practice as that of travelling at this early period of life (*WN*, 773–4).

As we have seen, at Glasgow Smith's reputation as a teacher and as author of *The Theory of Moral Sentiments* had gone some way to address the 'discredit' of university, to the extent that several aristocrats took the unusual step of sending their sons to study under Smith, and even, in the case of Thomas Fitzmaurice, to live with him. Why did Smith leave university to serve as Henry Scott's tutor and take him on a European tour?

It helped that the proposal came from Townshend, a rising politician whose erudition had impressed the learned societies of Edinburgh when he visited in 1759. During that summer Townshend travelled to Glasgow and met Smith, at which point they probably discussed the possibility of Smith taking the job when Henry was a bit older. Townshend had plans for Henry to follow him into politics, and chose Smith as one 'deeply read in the constitution and laws', 'ingenious, without being over-refin'd . . . general, without being too systematical', as Townshend put it in a letter to Henry.[1] Financially the terms of employment were attractive: £500 (around £31,000 today) a year during the tour itself, combined with an annuity giving an income of £300

(£19,000) for the rest of Smith's life. Without anyone other than his elderly mother to provide for, this would easily be enough to provide Smith with a comfortable lifestyle. Smith's income at Glasgow was partly dependent on fees paid by students, and hence varied between £150 and £300 (£10,000–20,000).

Although Smith ensured that his assistant Thomas Young delivered the rest of his course of lectures on jurisprudence, he insisted on repaying the fees his students had paid. They refused to accept reimbursement. As one recalled later:

> After warmly expressing his feelings of gratitude, and the strong sense he had of the regard shewn to him by his young friends, he told them, this was a matter between him and his own mind, and that he could not rest satisfied unless he performed what he deemed right and proper. 'You must not refuse me this satisfaction. Nay, by heavens, gentlemen, you shall not;' and seizing by the coat the young man who stood next to him, he thrust the money into his pocket, and then pushed him from him. The rest saw it was in vain to contest the matter, and were obliged to let him take his own way.[2]

Sadly this account of Professor Smith's manner with students is one of very few sources we have for thirteen years of lecturing. It depicts what was clearly not a routine interaction and suggests a profound mutual affection and respect that was probably unusual. It also shows Smith putting his moral philosophy into action; while he has satisfied his sense of professorial duty (the students will get the lectures they paid for), he finds himself called before a higher, more immediate authority. In saying that he had to settle with 'his own mind' it seems fair to assume that he was thinking of his 'impartial spectator'.

Smith and Buccleuch settled in Toulouse, where they spent eighteen months. The provincial city was probably chosen over Paris on the basis that the Duke was still too young and inexperienced to be exposed to the fleshpots and vice of the capital. Toulouse's *parlement* (law court) had a good library, if a poor reputation. In 1762 the court and the city as a whole had supported the judicial murder of a Protestant merchant, Jean Calas, charged with having murdered his own son to stop him converting to Catholicism. The authorities' failure to defend an innocent man against Roman Catholic fanaticism made the Calas Affair a cause célèbre for Enlightenment champions of religious toleration, notably Voltaire. In 1765, during Smith and Buccleuch's stay, Calas was posthumously declared innocent and the *parlement* seemed to swap craven obedience for something more assertive. It joined France's other *parlements* in refusing to register tax laws, even suggesting that in doing so they were defending the national interest against the despotism of Louis xv's ministers. In the short term, however, Smith and Buccleuch found themselves starved of company. This was probably not a problem for Smith, who was happy to use the

Jean-Baptiste Delafosse after Louis Carmontelle, *La Malheureuse Famille Calas*, 1765, etching with engraving. The Calas family in prison do not weep; in the face of persecution and death they exhibit self-command.

time to work on *The Wealth of Nations* (perhaps). But it did rob Buccleuch of the opportunity to practise his French and acquire the desired French polish. Buccleuch's younger brother Campbell Scott came over to keep him company. In April 1765 Townshend agreed that they could move, and after a tour of the south of France, the Pyrenees and two months in Geneva (where they met Voltaire) Smith and his party arrived in Paris in December 1765.

In Paris Smith would have encountered a city whose intellectual life was extremely lively, but very different from those of Glasgow and Edinburgh. The most obvious difference was that it was heterosocial rather than homosocial. In Britain, discussion of manners, ethics and other, more scientific, speculations went on in coffee houses, where the only female present was the 'Idol', who sat on a kind of enclosed throne at one end of the room, where she took orders and collected the money as well as many unsolicited attempts at gallantry by her clients. Here, male-only clubs met on a weekly or monthly basis. Like the fictional club celebrated in Richard Steele and Joseph Addison's periodical *The Spectator* (1711–12; an edition was in Smith's father's library), these clubs saw middle-class men of business, professionals and members of the aristocracy share opinions in a free-and-easy manner. Where inspiration failed, the plentiful supply of newspapers and pamphlets available provided food for thought and discussion. Although there were a handful of women-only clubs in London, women were generally excluded. While it was considered important for ladies to be able to participate in discussions among both men and women held around the domestic table, they had little freedom to lead the conversation or assert themselves. For parents of young girls, conversation was considered an art like piano-playing or watercolour painting, and was taught not as a means of self-expression but in order to appear fashionable and snag a wealthy husband for their daughter.

In Paris, intellectual discussion was centred on the *salons* led by aristocratic women such as the Duchesse d'Enville and other *salonnières*. These ladies were exceptionally well read and unafraid of exploring subjects that would have been entirely off-limits to their British equivalents, such as deism. Thanks to the writings of philosophers like Voltaire and Montesquieu, British religious practices, laws, social norms and particularly that curious entity known as the British constitution were topics of fashionable interest. British philosophers were much in demand in the 1760s. In 1763 the Peace of Paris had drawn the Seven Years War between Britain and France to an end. Many Frenchmen and women were shocked that Britain, a smaller nation with a lower population and an apparently unstable 'mixed' government (partly monarchical, partly aristocratic and partly democratic), could have defeated France so soundly, not only in Europe but in Canada, West Africa and India as well. The *salonnières'* Anglomania (which, despite the name, embraced Scottish culture as well) was further piqued by a patriotic desire to learn about how a rival power's institutions allowed her to leverage a smaller population and tap commercial wealth so as to project power across the globe.

There were limitations to this intellectual patronage, however. Some *salonnières* were motivated by a love of intellectual display and were more interested in being associated with the latest thinker than in exploring whether their ideas had more than mere novelty to recommend them. For those in fashion, the rewards were dizzying. These women were in a position not only to fund new publications or translations, but to ensure that the resulting edition sold well among other wealthy and influential people. They could ease their way into the highest circles at the court of King Louis xv at Versailles. Their praise was often fulsome, and in some cases combined with further, sexual, favours, which were gratifying in a different if particularly compelling way. But as with all fashions, intellectual tastes could change quickly. It might be fashionable for these nobles to appear to 'forget' their rank and esteem philosophers and poets without appearing to notice the latter's humbler social station. Nobles might toy with notions of meritocracy and a commercial nobility (unlike their British equivalents, the French aristocracy was prohibited from trade). Those thinkers who took this at face value or who took their speculations too far quickly learned that differences in rank remained important. A glance at the royal prisons of For-l'Évêque and the Bastille was a final reminder that, for all this speculation, France was an absolute monarchy. In the 1760s several authors of pamphlets on fiscal reform found themselves summarily arrested on a *lettre de cachet* (a royal warrant, which could not be challenged in the courts) and thrown into these prisons.

During Smith's tour his friend David Hume was in Paris, where he served as secretary to Lord Hertford, the British ambassador. Hume was carried away by the attentions he received in Paris and at Versailles. He wrote to Smith of his wonder. Could these be the same people 'that wou'd scarce show me common Civilities a very few Years ago at Edinburgh, who now receive me with such Applauses at Paris?' (c, 97). When Hume proposed to settle in Paris in 1765, Smith was quick to advise him against doing so. For all the 'boasted humanity and politeness' of the French, Smith found their friendship unreliable. 'They live in such large societies and their affections are dissipated among so great a variety of objects, that they can bestow but a very small share of them upon any individual.' He believed that 'the great Princes and Ladies who want you to live with them' were motivated not by genuine affection but 'vanity by having an illustrious man in their house' (c, 108). Hume risked becoming a kind of learned lapdog.

That is not to say that Smith was not excited and stimulated by the thinkers he met in France, or pleased by the attentions paid to him and *The Theory of Moral Sentiments*. The first, rather poor translation of *The Theory of Moral Sentiments* into French by Marc-Antoine Eidous appeared in 1764, as *La Métaphysique de l'âme* (The Metaphysics of the Soul). Hume claimed this translation had been

David Martin after Allan Ramsay, *David Hume*, mezzotint, 1767. This print shows a pleased-looking David Hume in a gold-laced coat.

read by Louis xv's learned and powerful mistress, the Marquise de Pompadour.[3] Smith seems to have been particularly taken with the *économistes*, a coven of thinkers on political economy who gathered around the royal physician François Quesnay. Quesnay had begun writing about the grain trade in the early 1750s, and Smith would have known his entries on 'Farmers' and 'Grain' for the famous encyclopaedia edited by Diderot and D'Alembert.

Quesnay understood agriculture to be the only source of a nation's wealth. Whereas agricultural outputs exceeded inputs, trade and manufactures brought no added value whatsoever: in the case of trade and manufacturing you only got out what you put in. Quesnay provided a diagram or 'Economic Table' that supposedly captured the French economy as a whole, showing how capital flowed between the agricultural, manufacturing and trade sectors. By the time he met Smith he had refined this table and was preparing to publish a book, whose title (*Physiocratie*) would give him and his disciples their more familiar name: the Physiocrats.

The grain trade in France was tightly regulated for political reasons, as the absolutist monarch feared that shortages of bread would lead to civil unrest. Quesnay urged the removal of these barriers to the free movement of grain. He also urged a radical simplification of the French tax system, a single 'royal tithe' on land taking the place of the web of taxes and dues that had built up over centuries and which varied from one part of the country to the other. Given the tax breaks awarded to the largest landholders (the Roman Catholic Church and the nobility) as well as vestiges of feudal dues paid in kind (including in some cases by so many days' labour a year), this was bound to be controversial – as much a social as a fiscal revolution. Quesnay acknowledged this, but breezily spoke of sweeping all resistance aside in an act of 'legal despotism'. As with his 'Table', Quesnay and the Physiocrats sought to reveal the simple mechanisms that they claimed created wealth. It was very much a case of an economy viewed from above, by technocrats who looked to the king to impose their measures on all his subjects.

The Physiocrats' approach was that of Enlightened despotism: the king's subjects were to be set free in a policy of laissez-faire (the phrase is said to have been coined by Jacques Vincent de Gournay, a Physiocrat), although the means chosen (royal edicts and intendants) were dictatorial, taking no notice of the fact that those affected might lack the information and understanding necessary to perceive how these measures would benefit either themselves or the public as a whole. In a cruel twist that hastened the end of the French monarchy, experiments with liberalization of the grain trade were indeed misunderstood by the general populace as a case of their royal 'father' removing his protection (against the widely held belief that the King would never allow his people to starve) in order to swell the profits of a new group of grain speculators and their get-rich-quick schemes. In a campaign of civil unrest known as the 'Grain War', placards appeared accusing the King of having himself become a grain speculator.[4]

Smith was clearly encouraged to find in the Physiocrats a group of like-minded men interested in sustained analysis of an entire economy. Since the 1690s English customs officials, philosophers and merchants had been publishing essays and pamphlets that launched a debate on important economic concepts such as the balance of trade and the role of money, but these had been journalistic rather than philosophical, discussing specific measures such as changes in the Bank of England's interest rate and proposed import or export tariffs on specific products. Quesnay and his allies represented something exciting for Smith. In the short term Smith may have been carried along by the neatness and beauty of the model presented on the 'Economic Table'. He later claimed that, had Quesnay lived long enough, he would have dedicated *The Wealth of Nations* to him. In the longer term, however, Smith came to a more critical view of the Physiocrats' excessive 'love of system'.

Although they are unlikely to have met in person, Smith's trip to France would also have encouraged him to engage with the thought of the philosopher Jean-Jacques Rousseau. Born in 1712 in Geneva to a line of watchmakers, Rousseau's restless mind and considerable pride had seen him bounce between a number of employments as tutor, composer and darling of the *salonnières*. He had also experienced several periods in exile: in 1765 he sought

Jean-Jacques Rousseau, the wild man of Geneva. David Martin after Allan Ramsay, *Jean Jacques Rousseau*, mezzotint, 1766.

refuge in England with the help of Hume, only to turn on his would-be benefactor in print the following year, accusing Hume of being part of a vast conspiracy against him. He had contributed the article on 'Political Economy' to the *Encyclopédie* in 1755, the same year his *Discourse on Inequality* appeared. Smith reviewed the latter for the *Edinburgh Review*, noting the ways in which Rousseau was developing arguments originally made by Mandeville.

Rousseau argued that mankind's advance from a state of natural independence, in which humans were solitary, amoral, 'dispersed in the woods . . . having no fixed habitation, and no need of each other's assistance', to a technologically advanced society founded on trade and co-dependence had seen savage virtue replaced with civilized exploitation.[5] Like Locke before him, Rousseau saw agriculture as the first stage in society, and so Rousseau imagined how the first property owner threw up a fence around a plot of what had been common land. 'The first man who, having enclosed a piece of ground, bethought himself of saying "This is mine", and found people simple enough to believe him, was the real founder of civil society.'[6]

> So long as [humans] undertook only what a single person could accomplish, and confined themselves to such arts as did not require the joint labour of several hands, they lived free, healthy, honest, and happy lives . . . But from the moment one man needed the help of another; from the moment it appeared advantageous to any one man to have enough provisions for two, equality disappeared, property was introduced, work became indispensable, and vast forests became smiling fields, which man had to water with the sweat of his brow, and where slavery and misery were soon seen to germinate and grow up with the crops.[7]

By goading and teasing us into the pursuit of consumer goods, the commercial society condemned us to sacrifice our happiness in chasing after pleasures that are forever beyond our reach.

Rousseau fully recognized that the division of labour boosted output and increased trading activity. The repetitiveness of the former, however, reduced people to the status of mere automatons, and our need to persuade others to enter into trade made us less genuine people – made us all actors whose smiling faces were masks. Unfortunately Rousseau was largely unable to come up with ways to escape this commercial society. An engraved illustration to the 1778 edition of the *Discourse* nonetheless showed a 'savage' man 'returning to his equals', disgusted by what he had seen of 'civilized' man. Smith clearly disagreed with Rousseau's argument that mankind entered a social state from a solitary 'state of nature'. As a species, *Homo sapiens* was inconceivable outside society. Even assuming human beings could survive outside society, as Rousseau claimed, they would not be able to conceive of a self without engaging in that trading of passions discussed in the previous chapters. To describe savage humans as entering society and 'beginning each to observe the others, and to desire to be observed himself' was profoundly misleading: without this mutual regard and sharing of passions there was no self and no human consciousness. Smith also recognized, correctly, that agriculture was not the first phase of society, but the third: the 'Age of Hunters' and 'Age of Shepherds' came before the 'Age of Agriculture'. Land became property only when previously nomadic tribes settled down, by a process in which tribal leaders granted land to their most important followers.

Without a 'pre-social' situation, there was no point reconstructing the thought processes that primordial men and women had gone through on the threshold of society. Smith pulled the rug out from under a raft of political thinkers who sought to understand government and sovereignty in terms of an 'original contract' made at this point in human history between ruler and ruled. Like Hume, Smith found it ludicrous that those alive today should be considered bound by such a contract, which could no longer be found as a physical document. Rather than trading certain pre-social rights ('natural rights') for a set of protections given by the ruler (a system of law and order, say), humans had never stood on a threshold separating 'nature' and 'civilization'. Smith's indifference to a language of natural or inalienable rights as well as

Il retourne chez ses Egaux.

Jean Dambrun after Clément-Pierre Marillier, *Il retourne chez ses Egaux, c.* 1783, etching with engraving. Disgusted with the depravity he finds among the 'civilized', Rousseau's noble savage returns to his forest.

a notion of consent in a contract between ruler and ruled continues to isolate him from much of the debate that goes on in politics.

While Rousseau insisted that humans had no instincts such as might distinguish them from other animals, Smith saw humans as distinguished by an inborn 'disposition to truck, barter and exchange' with each other that itself underlay the specialization of labour, some of whose benefits (increased production, improvement in quality) are obvious from the pin parable quoted in the Introduction. Smith would open *The Wealth of Nations* with this account of 'the causes of improvement', noting how the degree of labour specialization is limited by the size of the market. The larger the market, the greater the specialization. In a 'remote country' (that is, one that is geographically isolated), Smith noted, every man has to be brewer, baker and butcher to his family, because a small community cannot sustain a full-time baker, brewer or butcher. Specialization is also limited thanks to another problem with a barter economy: the fact that one cannot always be sure of finding someone willing to trade at the right time. The butcher has slaughtered a cow and has plenty of surplus meat that the baker would like to have. But the butcher does not need bread right now, and bread is all that the baker has to offer. The butcher will need bread next week, but by then the meat will have gone off, freezers not being available. 'They are all of them thus mutually less serviceable to one another' (*WN*, 37).

Hence the invention of money and its sole purpose as a store of value. You cannot eat money, nor can it clothe or house you. The value of money is what Smith calls 'exchange value', to differentiate it from 'value in use' (*WN*, 44). It is intrinsically worthless, and its value in exchange is based solely on custom, on loose consensus among a group of people that this particular thing will, to borrow a phrase printed on American dollar bills, serve as 'tender for all debts, public and private'. To make his point about the intrinsic worthlessness of money Smith notes the many different objects that have served as means of exchange in the past, including nails and lead bars. During the Siege of Montreal in 1760 those trapped inside the city used playing cards as currency.

Where money enables everyone to exchange their surplus, a web of interdependencies emerges that not only boosts output but improves quality of life, even for those at the bottom of a commercial society, who thus enjoy a standard of living superior to those at the pinnacle of a lower, earlier stage of social development, be that the first 'Age of Hunters' or the second 'Age of Shepherds'. It is notable how Smith describes the vast web of trading connections that the specialization of labour and free trade make possible. Spread across the entire globe, all these specialists nonetheless collaborate to provide for the common workman's needs. This web is obvious, Smith insists, asking us to join him inside 'the accommodation of the most common artificer or day-labourer in a civilized and thriving country'. He seizes on the worker's coat:

> The woollen coat, for example, which covers the day-labourer, as coarse and rough as it may appear, is the produce of the joint labour of a great multitude of workmen. The shepherd, the sorter of the wool, the wool-comber or carder, the dyer, the scribbler, the spinner, the weaver, the fuller, the dresser, with many others, must all join their different arts in order to complete even this homely production. How many merchants and carriers, besides, must have been employed in transporting the materials from some of the workmen to others who often live in a very distant part of the country! How much commerce and navigation in particular, how many ship-builders, sailors, sail-makers, rope-makers, must have been employed in order to bring together the different drugs made use of by the dyer, which often come from the remotest corners of the world! What a variety of labour too is necessary in order to produce the tools of the meanest of those workmen! (*WN*, 22–3)

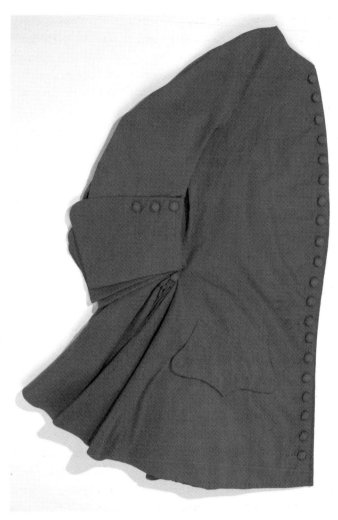

A very ordinary item of clothing: a British wool coat, *c.* 1740.

A laconic Scot with a dry sense of humour, Smith rarely gets excited. But here we have three exclamation marks in rapid succession. It is as if Smith is tugging our sleeve, struggling to contain his wonder at the fantastic vision summoned by the grubby overcoat slung over the back of a chair in a workman's hovel. He goes on to do the same with the tools lying about.

All this is possible when the division of labour and money make it worthwhile for individuals to create, accumulate and employ surplus 'stock', that is, capital (Smith uses both terms). In Rousseau's savage idyll there is no reason to do so:

> In that rude state of society in which there is no division of labour, in which exchanges are seldom made, and in which every man provides every thing for himself, it is not necessary that any stock should be accumulated or stored up beforehand in order to carry on the business of the society. Every man endeavours to supply by his own industry his own occasional wants as they occur. When he is hungry, he goes to the forest to hunt; when his coat is worn out, he cloaths himself with the skin of the first large animal he kills: and when his hut begins to go to ruin, he repairs it, as well as he can, with the trees and the turf that are nearest it (*WN*, 276).

The working man's accommodation, dress and other equipment may appear humble to us, but they exceed anything Rousseau's savage idyll could offer. Indeed, the working man's home is far better than 'that of many an African king, the absolute master of the lives and liberties of ten thousand naked savages' (*WN*, 24).

While Rousseau's stadial model of social development is declinist, going from best to worst, Smith's model of 'the natural Progress of Opulence' presumes that human society is designed to draw mankind together and improve quality of life for all, as a 'subsistence' lifestyle gives way to ones characterized by 'conveniency' and eventually 'luxury'. The natural order has 'the cultivation and improvement of the country' leading the way, as only the country can provide the means of subsistence. Manufacturing, and therefore cities, can only grow when there is a large enough surplus of capital to invest in the 'conveniencies' and 'luxuries' that the former provide. Given the security of agriculture as a pursuit, few would, if given the choice, elect to invest their time and capital in manufactures, let alone in trade, where one's capital is not under one's own 'view and command' (*WN*, 377).

The progress of opulence from agriculture to manufactures and then to foreign trade has been traced in 'every growing society' (*WN*, 380). But in 'the modern states of Europe' this order was inverted. This was because of the perverse incentives that operated under the feudal system, which emerged after the collapse of the Roman empire. Feudal lords oppressed their tenants, robbing them of security and hence discouraging them from improving their land. Restrictions on the movement of grain prevented those who were nonetheless able to produce a surplus from selling it. Naturally, the more enterprising fled to the cities, giving an artificial boost to manufacture and foreign trade. Cities secured further rights for themselves from the king (the biggest lord, in other words) in exchange for supporting them financially as they attempted to put the smaller lords in their place. Far from the countryside improving the city, as the 'natural progress of opulence' mandated, the city improved the country, as its merchants bought estates and introduced improved farming methods as well as 'order and good government' among country-dwellers who had previously 'lived almost in a continual state of war with their neighbours' (*WN*, 412).

The most important result of this inversion occurred when the feudal lords encountered the luxuries produced by the city's manufactories and by foreign trade, something that could not have occurred had the natural order been followed. The expected process was short-circuited. 'In a country which has neither foreign commerce, nor any of the finer manufactures', Smith notes, 'a great proprietor, having nothing for which he can exchange the greater part of the produce of his lands which is over and above the maintenance of the cultivators, consumes the whole in rustick hospitality at home' (*WN*, 412–13). Hence the vast banqueting halls found in castles, as well as the hospitality of Arab princes. Such lords lived surrounded by an army of retainers, for lack of anything else on which to spend the rents paid them by their tenants. Though these retainers were regularly let off their rents when they couldn't pay and enjoyed free food, this bounty depended entirely on the 'good pleasure' of the lord, who, like the aforementioned 'African King', had his retainers' property and lives at his command (*WN*, 415). When he went to war with a neighbouring lord his retainers went too, and did the fighting and dying for him.

The lords were 'masters of mankind' and hence followed the usual 'vile maxim': 'All for ourselves, and nothing for other people.' But this changed once foreign trade and manufacture provided these masters with luxury goods, that is, 'with something for which they could exchange the whole surplus produce of their lands, and which they could consume themselves without sharing either with tenants or retainers'. Smith is dismissive of the bargain these lords struck: 'For a pair of diamond buckles perhaps, or for something as frivolous and useless . . . for the gratification of the most childish, the meanest and the most sordid of all vanities, they gradually bartered their whole power and authority' (*WN*, 418–19). The knock-on effects were profound for the retainers, who were let go. Eager to increase his rental income, the lord agreed to give his tenants longer and more secure tenure in return for investment in improvements to the land (fertilizer, drainage, better breeds of sheep, and so on) that would allow them to produce more and afford a higher rent.

Without subservient hangers-on willing to risk their necks for their lords, the lords' ability to oppose 'the regular execution of justice' and engage in pointless yet violent feuding was curtailed: 'A regular government was established in the country as well as in the city, nobody having sufficient power to disturb its operations in the one, any more than in the other.' Though the supply of free food had ended, the former retainers now enjoyed security and tranquillity, along with a better quality of life. A 'revolution' was thus brought about by two classes of people 'who had not the least intention to serve the publick' (*WN*, 421, 422). A similar shift had also robbed the priests of their authority. Struck by the hypocrisy of priests preaching humility while practising luxury, 'the inferior ranks of people no longer looked upon that order, as they had done before, as the comforters of their distress, and the relievers of their indigence' (*WN*, 804). Although Hume agreed with this view in *The History of England*, published in 1754–61, today's medieval historians would strongly dispute Smith's explanation for the decline of feudalism. It is nonetheless clear that Smith sees the study of history

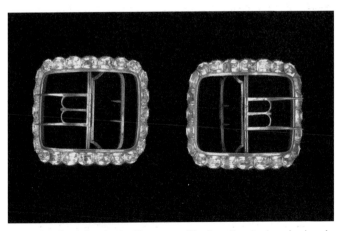

A pair of steel and glass shoe buckles, *c.* 1780s. Thanks to Georgian 'populuxe' goods, 'middling' folk in Britain could strut like lords.

as highly important to understanding 'the nature and causes of the wealth of nations'.

As already noted, Smith came from a Scottish tradition of stadial thinking, of a kind that would strike us today as more anthropological than historical. In the case of this feudal revolution, however, the expected 'natural progress of opulence' was 'inverted': 'history' and 'nature' were running in opposite directions. Rather than downplaying this or being frustrated by human society's failure to follow the script, Smith draws attention to the ways in which the same state of 'commercial society' has been achieved by different routes. This allows him to emphasize the role played by unintended consequences. Smith is surprisingly comfortable with this – more comfortable, perhaps, than many other historians. Though the 'natural' route is logical and shorter, there are other ways of reaching the 'civilized' commercial state. These routes were not mapped out in advance, however. The 'great proprietors' and the 'merchants and artificers' were motivated not by a desire 'to serve the publick' but by 'vanity' and commercial 'interest' respectively (*wn*, 422).

Although Smith does not refer to the 'invisible hand' here, otherwise this historical account of the decline of feudalism bears a strong resemblance to the explanation in *The Theory of Moral Sentiments* of how our admiration for the trappings of wealth is made 'to serve the publick' in a similar, equally unintended fashion. Here Smith again describes how, as in the case of the Poor Man's Son, 'the pleasures of wealth and greatness . . . strike the imagination as something grand and beautiful and noble, of which the attainment is well worth all the toil and anxiety which we are so apt to bestow upon it.' We admire the 'rich and the great', Smith insists, not because we suppose them to be happier than us, but because we imagine that 'they possess more means of happiness' (*tms*, 183, 182). They appear to live surrounded by gadgets carefully and ingenuously designed to serve their every need, including needs we didn't know we had. These objects serve utility, but it is clearly a 'frivolous utility', as the benefits they offer do not justify the costs in anxiety. Far from satisfying the possessor, these gadgets defer the enjoyment of those simple pleasures that the vast majority of us have immediately to hand.

In his review of Rousseau's *Discourse on Inequality* Smith had quoted a passage referring to how 'the vast forrests of nature were changed into agreeable plains'. There is an echo of this in Smith's famous 'invisible hand' passage from *The Theory of Moral Sentiments*, which argues against Rousseau's claim that the creation of private property and the emergence of insatiable desires for luxuries left the majority of mankind worse off than when they wandered the forests alone. Far from cursing us with a false perception of 'the pleasures of wealth and greatness',

> it is well that nature imposes upon us in this manner. It is this deception which rouses and keeps in continual motion the industry of mankind. It is this which first prompted them to cultivate the ground, to build houses, to found cities and commonwealths, and to invent and improve all the sciences and arts, which ennoble and embellish human life; which have entirely changed the whole face of the globe, have turned the rude forests of nature into agreeable and fertile plains, and made the trackless and barren ocean a new fund of subsistence, and the great high road of communication to the different nations of the earth. The earth by these labours of mankind has been obliged to redouble her natural fertility, and to maintain a greater multitude of inhabitants (*TMS*, 183–4).

Though 'the proud and unfeeling landlord' imagines he can consume the produce of his vast estates, his eyes are literally bigger than his stomach, which is the same size as that of the lowliest peasant tilling his fields. Like the feudal lord, he is therefore obliged to share the rest with others. Despite 'their own vain and insatiable desires' and their 'natural selfishness and rapacity',

> they are led by an invisible hand to make nearly the same distribution of the necessaries of life, which would have been made, had the earth been divided into equal portions among all its inhabitants, and thus without intending it, without knowing it, advance the interest of the society, and afford means to the multiplication of the species. When Providence divided the earth among a few lordly masters, it neither forgot nor abandoned those who seemed to have been left out in the partition. These last too enjoy their share of all that it produces. In what constitutes the real happiness of human life, they are in no respect inferior to those who would seem so much above them. In ease of body and peace of mind, all the different ranks of life are nearly upon a level, and the beggar, who suns himself by the side of the highway, possesses that security which kings are fighting for (*TMS*, 184–5).

Smith's encounter with the Physiocrats and Rousseau must have encouraged him to write his treatise on 'the nature and causes of the wealth of nations', a kind of book that had not been attempted in English before. These thinkers also demonstrated the risks of seeing human interaction in a commercial society either as a machine that could be reprogrammed from above (as Quesnay saw it) or as irredeemably corrupt (as Rousseau did). Quesnay and Rousseau had very different views about the overall arc of human history: while the former saw human society as perfectible through top-down intervention, Rousseau saw human society as doomed to search in vain for a way back to a savage perfection. Yet both viewed human passions as obstacles to that perfection, whether as grit in the cogs of the machine or as self-destructive impulses.

Smith recognized that, for all the hand-wringing over the supposed corruption of a commercial society, nobody wanted to return to the forest – even assuming that was possible, which it was not. Whether the route followed was 'natural' or 'historic', human society was destined to follow the 'progress of opulence'. On one, historical plane, this progress led from the forest to the 'fertile plains' and from slavish dependence of the majority on a few tyrannizing 'masters of mankind' to a modern world, in which the majority are dependent on the majority. After the 'revolution' ended feudalism there were still, of course, landlords and tenants, and now the 'artificers' who provided the landlords with all their 'trinkets of frivolous utility'. Here Rousseau saw only an artificial and destructive inequality. Smith pointed to the very real improvements in the quality of clothing, housing and even luxuries enjoyed by even the humblest 'day-labourer', which brought a level of comfort unknown in the forest. He also pointed to the greater freedom enjoyed by the majority.

Whereas before the 'masters of mankind' had the property and very lives of their tenants and other dependants at their command, now the situation was very different: the tenant would pay his rent, but would not follow his landlord into battle. The 'artificer' was even more free, as he earned his living 'not of one, but of a hundred or a thousand different customers. Though in some measure obliged to them all, therefore, he is not absolutely dependent upon any one of them' (wn, 420). An innate 'disposition to truck, barter and exchange' led to the specialization of labour, which in turn drove a 'progress of opulence' towards a commercial society in which everyone was interdependent and enjoyed ample means of achieving a standard of living that provided not only mere 'subsistence', but even a degree of 'luxury' as well.

Put that way, the human condition seems rather pleasant. We can, it seems, sit back and let nature take its course. Though human society is an 'immense fabric', 'To raise and support [it] seems in this world, if I may say so, to have been the peculiar and darling care of Nature' (*TMS*, 86). This 'care' is seen in the innate desires and dispositions shared by all human beings. The story of the eclipse of feudal society even suggests that where this 'progress' goes off-track, the 'invisible hand' will eventually return us to the correct path. This path will lead to greater 'freedom' as well as greater 'communication' between different parts of the globe. International trade, after all, is 'intended' to foster peace and understanding among nations. Yet we are still left with serious concerns. The day-labourer may wear a nice coat, but is the life of endless, repetitive, monotonous work to which he and everyone else is condemned by the specialization of labour a price worth paying? Our dignity seems compromised by this apparently beneficial 'exchange'.

There is something equally undignified in Smith's suggestion that we are victims of a 'delusion', and that this is a good thing. It is part of the big plan. But what if our desire to emulate the great leads us to emulate their morality as well as their consumption of 'trinkets of frivolous utility'? And whose plan is this anyway? Are Smith's 'Nature' and 'Providence' the same as 'God', and, if so, what kind of God would manipulate us by delusions and invisible hands? The Enlightenment project aimed to set humans free from the superstitions and false idols to which we willingly outsource our destinies. Smith seems to be asking us to trust a new idol. As for Smith's notion of 'peaceful commerce' (*la douce commerce*, an idea he picked up from Montesquieu), this, too, seems unbelievable. Trade has often been the cause of international jealousy and in many cases armed conflict. We often find ourselves speaking of commerce as a matter of winners and losers. It is these challenges which remain to be addressed.

4

Golden Dreams, 1767–75

Adam Smith's letter of 1765 advising Hume against settling in Paris
suggests that, after a year in the city, Smith was getting somewhat
homesick. As it happens, his stay on the Continent would not last
as long as originally planned. In August 1766 Buccleuch fell ill after
hunting with the French court at Compiègne. Though he recovered,
his younger brother Campbell later suffered a similar bout of sickness,
which in his case was fatal. On 1 November 1766 Smith and Buccleuch
landed at Dover with Campbell Scott's body. Smith's nursing of both
boys had been exemplary. He had been able to call on Quesnay, Louis
xv's physician, for medical advice. There is no sense that Smith was
held accountable by the Scott family or by Buccleuch. The death cut
short their tour, however, with the result that Smith spent the winter
of 1766–7 in London, awaiting Buccleuch's coming of age. In September
1767 Smith duly accompanied Buccleuch on his formal entry to his
Scottish territories, which was also the Duke's first trip north of
the border. Despite various requests to accompany other young
aristocrats on their tours, Smith never crossed the Channel again.
As he had noted to Hume in 1765, 'A man is always displaced in a
forreign Country' (c, 108).

Buccleuch set about introducing a number of reforms to his
family's vast estates, reforms which Smith probably inspired, or
at very least discussed with his former pupil on visits to Dalkeith,
the Buccleuch family seat south of Edinburgh. These were intended
to encourage investment in improvements such as new crops,

marling (a kind of fertilizer), improved breeds of sheep, better drainage, afforestation in order to grow trees for timber and the creation of water meadows and roads. They included removing restrictions on the sale and lease of land such as entail, the legal device by which noble houses protected the integrity of their lands across the generations, ensuring that they could not be broken up by dissolute descendants (like Buccleuch's grandfather Francis Scott, the spendthrift 2nd Duke). Between one-third and half of all land in Scotland was entailed in Smith's day. An entail prevented descendants from selling the land in question or even offering a tenant a long lease. It thus 'locked up' a vast amount of land; as Smith stated, 'it excludes lands intirely from commerce' (*LJ*, 70). This naturally denied it any 'value in exchange' and kept it in the hands of the 'great proprietors' (whom Smith claims were rarely interested in improving the land) rather than allowing it to be sold to more entrepreneurial individuals (who could introduce improvements, boosting the land's productivity).

In *The Wealth of Nations* Smith describes entail as demonstrating how 'laws frequently continue in force long after the circumstances, which first gave occasion to them, and which could alone render them reasonable, are no more.' In feudal times, when 'great landed estates were a sort of principalities', entail provided a certain amount of security for the lords' thousands of retainers, by preventing any one lord from breaking up what was a kind of petty state (*WN*, 383, 384). Now that feudal lords had traded their 'principalities' for 'trinkets of frivolous utility', law and order was provided by the state, and entail's advantages no longer outweighed its disadvantages as an obstacle to agricultural improvement. The only justification Smith could find for their continuation was as a means of ensuring that the aristocracy would retain sufficient wealth to continue asserting their claim to a monopoly of high state office and other privileges. Smith's response to this makes his disdain for aristocratic privilege clear:

Entails, however, are still respected through the greater part of Europe, in those countries particularly in which noble birth is a necessary qualification for the enjoyment either of civil or military honours. Entails are thought necessary for maintaining this exclusive privilege of the nobility to the great offices and honours of their country; and that order having usurped one unjust advantage over the rest of their fellow-citizens, lest their poverty should render it ridiculous, it is thought reasonable that they should have another (*WN*, 384–5).

To help them set rents, Buccleuch's managers collected statistics on sheep farming and worked out a formula by which the Duke could use current wool and wedder lamb (castrated male lambs) prices to work out the value of his sheep farms. Buccleuch advertised all 439 farm tenancies in the *Edinburgh Advertiser*, inviting those interested in renting any specific farm to apply in writing, indicating what improvements they proposed to make. The successful bidders were to receive longer tenancies, allowing them more time to recoup their investment, as well as the promise of having the money they had spent on improvements paid back if their tenancy was terminated by Buccleuch.

The reforms came as a shock to many local families, who had been tenants to various dukes for generations. The suspicions of tenants made it necessary to collect the aforementioned data by covert means. Though they were eventually pushed through, the reforms were still not fully implemented when Smith died in 1790, and would not have worked had Buccleuch not shown an equally Smithian willingness to shoulder the non-economic burdens of being a laird: abandoning Townshend's dream of a political career, living full-time at Dalkeith (instead of in London) and creating a volunteer militia. Buccleuch thus managed to implement reforms while remaining 'clan chief' and 'father of his tenantry'.

This was clearly 'top-down' agricultural improvement, but the programme was not imposed at a single blow, nor was the programme a crudely capitalistic one intended to replace the web of connections tying laird and tenant together. Pecuniary interest alone did not drive Buccleuch; rents were often set at a level slightly below the 'bid' made by would-be tenants, it being recognized that high rents would rob 'his tenants of the hopes of bettering their situation in life'. Though by no means a philosopher, Buccleuch's manager, William Keir, was Smithian enough to note that such hopes represented 'one of the strongest motives to industry and exertion' and that when rents were set at the highest level possible, 'the Country is also deprived of the benifit of that part of their labour which they would otherwise have bestowed upon the cultivation and improvement of their farms.'[1] Or, as Smith put it:

> the liberal [i.e. generous] reward of labour, as it encourages the propagation, so it increases the industry of the common people. The wages of labour are the encouragement of industry, which, like every other human quality, improves in proportion to the encouragement it receives. A plentiful subsistence increases the bodily strength of the labourer, and the comfortable hope of bettering his condition, and of ending his days perhaps in ease and plenty, animates him to exert that strength to the utmost. Where wages are high, accordingly, we shall always find the workmen more active, diligent, and expeditious, than where they are low (*wn*, 99).

In one of his many additions to the sixth edition of *The Theory of Moral Sentiments* (1790), Smith included a critique of the 'Man of System', noting how 'He seems to imagine that he can arrange the different members of a great society with as much ease as the hand arranges the different pieces upon a chess-board', when the reality was that 'in the great chess-board of human society, every single piece has a principle of motion of its own' (*TMS*, 234). Unlike Quesnay, who treated the French king's subjects as if they were unthinking pawns, Buccleuch's managers sought to understand the 'principles of motion' of their tenants, and to harness them in the long-term interest of 'the Country'. Alongside a desire to 'better their Situation', Buccleuch's acknowledgement and development of age-old non-economic (social, moral) ties linking him with his tenants also drew on non-economic 'principles of motion'. Chief among these was Scottish patriotism. Even in the twenty-first century it is evident that this force remains strong, and surprisingly indifferent to economic self-interest.

After seeing Buccleuch installed at Dalkeith, Smith returned to Kirkcaldy and was reunited with his mother. He remained there from May 1767 until 1773, working on *The Wealth of Nations*. He wrote to Hume in June 1767, describing his life there as divided between 'My Business', which consisted of 'Study in which I have been very deeply engaged for about a Month past', and 'My Amusements', which consisted of 'long, solitary walks by the Sea side'. 'You may judge how I spend my time', he wrote, but by his own estimation he felt himself 'extremely happy, comfortable and contented. I never was, perhaps, more so in all my life' (*c*, 125). In *The Theory of Moral Sentiments* Smith notes that avarice, ambition and vainglory each lead us to overestimate the difference between poverty and riches, between low and high office or rank and between obscurity and fame. An inflated sense of the rewards leads us to take risks that bear little relation to the actual benefits we might, if we are lucky, end up enjoying: 'Wherever prudence does not direct, wherever justice does not permit, the attempt to change our situation, the man who does attempt it, plays at the most unequal of all games of hazard, and stakes every thing against scarce any thing.'

Rather than taking his word for this, Smith asks us to consider 'what has happened within the circle of your own experience'. If we do this, he predicts, we will find that 'the misfortunes of by far the greater part of them have arisen from their not knowing when they were well, when it was proper for them to sit still and to be contented' (*TMS*, 149–50). Smith's letter makes it clear that at the age of 44 he was able to appreciate the advantages of his situation and resist the urge to compare his simple life in Kirkcaldy unfavourably with the busyness of Edinburgh, where Hume was then living. Smith not only knew he possessed the means to be happy in his current situation, he actually was 'extremely happy'. This 'real happiness' was one 'we have at all times at hand, and in our power' and that is based on pleasures 'almost always the same' as those we can imagine enjoying 'in the most glittering and exalted situation that our idle fancy can hold out to us'. Alongside his walks, Smith clearly saw time spent drinking with friends (being 'good company over a bottle') as one source of 'real happiness' that we have always at hand (*TMS*, 150).

The restless speculation of less tranquil minds, however, continued to provide Smith with plenty to ponder on his long walks on the beach. On 25 June 1772 Ayr Bank (formally known as Douglas, Heron & Co.) suspended payments, going bankrupt with liabilities exceeding £1 million (around £64 million in today's money).[2] The bank had been established in the Scottish city of Ayr in 1769, and was intended to fund agricultural improvements of the kind Buccleuch was trying to encourage through his reforms. Indeed, Buccleuch himself subscribed £1,000 of the bank's founding capital of £96,000 (around £6 million in today's money). The creation of this and other banks grew out of dissatisfaction with the two chartered banks, the Bank of Scotland and the Royal Bank of Scotland (RBS), established in 1695 and 1727, respectively. Scottish savers simply did not have enough capital to invest in all the infrastructure, agricultural, industrial and housing projects under way in Scotland the 1760s. These included the Forth and Clyde Canal; the construction of Edinburgh's New Town; expanding linen production; shipbuilding (for the linen export trade); and the opening of factories like the Carron Ironworks, established in 1759, which provided parts for James Watts's pioneering steam engines and also supplied the Royal Navy with artillery. Capital markets were therefore tight, meaning it was difficult to get capital without paying high levels of interest. RBS was failing the Scottish economy, it was said, by failing to give credit on 'easy' terms.

Frustrated entrepreneurs turned to money brokers for capital. Many of them lent capital in the form of phoney bills of exchange produced by a practice known as 'drawing and redrawing', by which two parties located in separate cities could create capital out of thin air by repeatedly exchanging short-term (two months, say) IOUs with each other, without either side having in fact lent any equivalent sum or provided any goods or services of an equivalent value. Promissory notes between merchants and tradesmen circulated widely in the late eighteenth-century economy, almost as another form of cheque (like cheques, they could be 'endorsed' on the back, and so pass to a third, fourth or fifth party). For those in on the fraud, this game of 'pass the parcel' was a profitable endeavour, in the short term at least: one partner secured commission and interest for the loan of capital they did not in fact have, while the other was able to exchange the note for real goods and services (at the usual discount for such bills of exchange).

Such practices made RBS even more wary of accepting promissory notes, increasing demands for a more 'patriotic' bank willing to inject fresh capital into the Scottish economy by granting cash accounts, loans and printing its own banknotes. This is what Ayr Bank did: it was founded 'for the express purpose of relieving the distress of the country' (WN, 313). The illustration on page 129 is only the right half of the note; to the left of the black band would have been another half with the same information, like the counterfoil to a cheque. When it was issued to Will Hay this note was cut in half in a wavy line: the wave in the line as well as the printed black pattern were intended to prevent forgery (as a forged note would not 'line up' with the edge of the bank's half of the note). The named bearer (Will Hay) and the counterfoil might well remind us of a personal cheque, though today they are rapidly passing out of use. But, of course, all paper money is essentially a cheque: like this Ayr note, they have a signature and a date. The main differences are the vastly improved anti-forgery devices and the fact that the cheque is made out to 'the bearer', rather than a named individual.

To us the idea of banks other than a central bank such as the Bank of England issuing banknotes seems strange. Until the 1825 Bank Charter Act all British banks could print their own banknotes, a situation rife with danger, in so far as a 'run' on one bank could and did spread to others that handled its notes. All those handling the notes needed to be in a position to gauge the creditworthiness not of one central bank (backed by the government), but of twenty or thirty. Even more odd from a contemporary perspective is the fact that many such banknotes had option clauses that gave the bank issuing them the option to refuse to pay 'on demand' (that is, to hand over the sum printed on the paper note) and instead convert the note into an interest-bearing six-month loan. An act of parliament in 1765 had prohibited the use of option clauses on notes of £1 or less, but they continued to be used for larger denomination notes.

Unfortunately, Ayr Bank's generosity in giving its own subscribers loans, in issuing loans and in accepting the loans of other banks (a practice known as discounting) led it to overreach itself by lending to a series of projects of an equally speculative nature. For example, though there had been signs of a glut in linen markets in late 1769, investment in linen production continued. In order to continue making payments in exchange for notes Ayr Bank had to borrow money in London at 8 per cent, when the rate it was getting from its own loans was just 3 per cent. Its generosity led it to accept spurious bills and, indeed, to engage in its own 'drawing and redrawing' on London. A situation emerged in which risks were not 'priced'

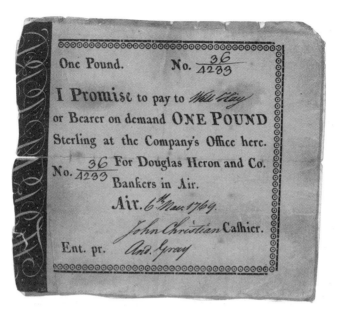

One Pound.   No. 36/4233

I Promise to pay to *Will Hay*
or Bearer on demand ONE POUND
Sterling at the Company's Office here.

No. 36/4233 For Douglas Heron and Co.
Bankers in Air.

Air. 6th Nov 1769.

John Christian Cashier.

Ent. pr. *And. Gray*

Banking on Air.

– were not in fact taken into consideration – because everyone was
confident of their own ability to sell the doubtful bills and notes
before disaster struck; that is, that they would not find themselves
in a liquidity trap, unable to find takers for the bills and notes. In
1771 political unrest in the American colonies began to make those
involved in linen exports nervous. Though the collapse was by this
point inevitable, the trigger came the following June, when a London
bank, Neal, James, Fordyce & Down (to which Ayr was heavily
exposed), collapsed.

Englishmen of course suspected a plot by those canny Scots. 'The
deel away wi ye all ye English Pudding boys ken ye nae that Paper is
lighter of digestion than Gold', cries the Scot on the broomstick in
the London satire reproduced here, as he zooms back to Scotland
with bags full of English gold, leaving chaos and destruction in his
wake. In reality the crash caused even more damage north of the

border. Instead of 'relieving the distress of the country', Ayr Bank ended up making it much, much worse. As Hume noted in a letter to Smith of 27 June 1772, this distress was not limited to the country around Ayr. It spread across Scotland and threatened the English banking system itself, 'stopping' banks (that is, causing them to stop paying gold in return for their own notes) across the United Kingdom and threatening large industrial concerns such as the Carron Ironworks:

> We are here in a very melancholy Situation: Continual Bankruptcies, universal Loss of Credit, and endless Suspicions . . . The Case is little better in London . . . even the Bank of England is not entirely free from Suspicion. Those of Newcastle, Norwich, and Bristol are said to be stopp'd: The Thistle Bank has been reported to be in the same Condition: The Carron Company is reeling, which is one of the greatest Calamities of the whole; as they gave Employment to near 10,000 People. Do these Events any-wise affect your Theory? (c, 162)

The collapse of Ayr Bank in 1772: those canny Scots dump worthless paper on the London market and escape with their ill-gotten gold. Anonymous, *A View of the Deluge of Scotch Paper Currency for English Gold*, 1772, etching.

Work constructing the Forth and Clyde Canal was suspended. Twenty-seven of the thirty Scottish banks in existence went under. It took three years for the Scottish economy as a whole to recover.

For Smith's patron the crash was personally and financially very embarrassing. After the Bank of England refused to take on more Ayr notes (it already had £300,000 worth), Buccleuch and other subscribers decided to try to prop up Ayr Bank rather than declaring bankruptcy. In order to be in a position to reopen the bank in September 1772, they had to issue £350,000 of redeemable annuities secured against their estates, at an eye-watering 15 per cent interest. Though these were converted in 1774 into bonds secured on Buccleuch's entailed lands, the process dragged on until 1804 and pushed less wealthy landed aristocratic investors in the bank to the wall. If Buccleuch was acting on Smith's advice, it was very poor advice indeed. Whether out of patriotism or a sense of responsibility, Buccleuch's recourse to annuities and bonds increased his liability from £4,400 (around £280,000) in 1772 to £79,666 (£2.5 million) in 1795.[3]

And what of Smith's 'Theory'? Smith held that any bank that 'understood and attended to its own particular interest' would soon learn not to issue more capital than 'the country can easily absorb and employ' (*wn*, 302). Whereas it could normally issue paper to four times its cash reserves (that is, gold and silver, in coin of the realm), any paper issued above the country's capacity would immediately come back for exchange into coin. Contrary to 'the wishes of those' who complained of the 'distress' caused by tight credit, the job of the banking sector was not to add to the capital of the country, but to render 'a greater part of that capital active and productive than would otherwise be so'. Any capital that men of business had to keep in the form of gold or silver was 'dead stock, which, so long as it remains in this situation, produces nothing either to him or to his country'. This gold and silver is not a productive investment but simply a convenient form of transferring capital from one productive activity to another. Smith compares it to a 'highway'.

Roads are needed in order to carry grain to market. But they take up land that could be used to grow something, or as pasture for sheep. What if the farmer could transport his grain to market by air, by balloon, say? The roads could be turned into fields. By issuing paper notes, banks created 'a sort of waggon-way through the air'. Smith conceded that commerce and industry were not quite as safe when, 'as it were, suspended upon the Daedalian wings of paper money' (*WN*, 321), referring to Daedalus, the architect and inventor who according to myth escaped the labyrinth of Minos by making sets of wings for himself and his son, Icarus. Unfortunately Icarus was carried away by his new-found ability to fly and ascended too high, whereupon the sun's rays melted the wax holding his wings together and he fell into the sea. Though Smith's wings are not 'Icarian', the warning is clear.

Paper money could increase the speed of circulation to such an extent that individuals might no longer feel it necessary to pause to work out the value of a specific bill or piece of paper, either because they had no intention to hold it for very long or because they were convinced that a 'sucker' could be found whose ignorance or credulity could be relied upon to make them buy that piece of paper. It might even create a situation in which all those involved in the game of musical chairs were aware that the music would stop eventually and that the notes they were circulating were of uncertain value. Nobody could behave in a way that suggested that they acknowledged these truths, however. Suddenly to refuse to discount the notes would unleash a panic that would have everyone running for the door at the same time. Banks had to reduce their exposure slowly. Happily, the stupidity of Ayr Bank's directors in failing to perceive 'scarce any distinction between real and circulating bills' (that is, real bills and those produced by 'drawing and redrawing') enabled their rival banks to 'get very easily out of that fatal circle, from which they could not otherwise have disengaged themselves without incurring a considerable loss, and perhaps too even some degree of discredit' (*WN*, 313, 315).

There was, perhaps, a rationale behind continuing to pass the parcel, as Smith conceded:

> Though the drawer, acceptor, and endorsers of the bill should, all of them, be persons of doubtful credit; yet still the shortness of the date [i.e. of the loan period] gives some security to the owner of the bill. Though all of them may be very likely to become bankrupts, it is a chance if they all become so in so short a time. The house is crazy, says a weary traveller to himself, and will not stand very long; but it is a chance if it falls to-night, and I will venture, therefore, to sleep in it to-night (*WN*, 309).

One of the most worrying indicators of a lack of confidence during the 2008 banking crisis was the tripling in the rate at which London banks lent each other money overnight, the LIBOR (London Interbank Offered Rate). Confidence was so bad that Smith's 'weary travellers' would not stay in a house they considered 'crazy' (that is, full of cracks and flaws), not even for a single night.

Far from arguing that the market could be trusted to price the value of each and every bank's notes, Smith advocated a ban on such option clauses and wanted to restrict banks other than the Bank of England from issuing notes below a certain value. The latter would help restrict their circulation to larger enterprises and the money market itself, where people were better informed as to the risks involved in accepting such notes. Such regulations were compared by Smith to the building codes imposed on London in the wake of the Great Fire of 1666:

> To restrain private people, it may be said, from receiving in payment the promissory notes of a banker, for any sum

whether great or small, when they themselves are willing to receive them; or, to restrain a banker from issuing such notes, when all his neighbours are willing to accept of them, is a manifest violation of that natural liberty which it is the proper business of law, not to infringe, but to support. Such regulations may, no doubt, be considered as in some respect a violation of natural liberty. But those exertions of the natural liberty of a few individuals, which might endanger the security of the whole society, are, and ought to be, restrained by the laws of all governments; of the most free, as well as of the most despotical. The obligation of building party walls, in order to prevent the communication of fire, is a violation of natural liberty, exactly of the same kind with the regulations of the banking trade which are here proposed (*wn*, 324).

As noted elsewhere, Smith rarely refers to universal concepts of justice in any of his writings. When he does make use, as here, of phrases such as 'natural liberty', such liberties or 'sacred rights of mankind' are usually under assault. Whenever they are not being threatened by mercantilism or government intervention, Smith prefers to keep silent. It is striking that here Smith insists that these restraints on individual liberty are justified by their contribution to the 'security of the whole society'.

But how can such restraints be policed? The Great Fire of London had focused attention on the need for building regulations, and the 1667 London Building Act and its amendments contained detailed prescriptions. A five-storey brick building had to have a party wall two bricks thick up to the first floor, and one and a half bricks thick up to the garret. The wall also had to separate the roof space from that of the houses on either side. Though including such walls gave bricklayers around three weeks' extra employment and required 32,000 'extra' bricks (thus stimulating the economy), for the speculative builders behind the construction of the majority of new terraced housing in areas such as Spitalfields (in London) this was a significant extra cost.

Party walls are by their nature invisible, and inevitably some builders did not build them, though stiffer penalties and more regulations were introduced under another Building Act in 1774. The fact remains that few residents would have known if the house they lived in had party walls or not. Fire insurance had been around since the 1690s, and in Smith's day each company had their own fire engines, which would put out fires only in houses that had a plaque bearing the logo of their firm on the facade. The free market might have incentivized builders to build party walls, through reduced insurance premiums. Unfortunately, as Smith himself noted, 'taking the whole kingdom at an average, nineteen houses in twenty, or rather perhaps ninety-nine in a hundred, are not insured from fire'.

The City (as in its buildings and people, rather than merely its financial institutions) remained exposed to a catastrophic risk. Yet rather than basing the decision to insure or not on 'nice calculation' of risk, most residents did nothing, out of 'mere thoughtless rashness and presumptuous contempt of the risk' (wn, 126). Thus while Smith clearly feels that regulation is necessary to protect 'society as a whole' by restraints on the free actions of individuals where those actions can cause widespread devastation, his choice of analogy only highlights the real problems with implementing this kind of regulation. It is nonetheless striking that, when 'natural liberty' and 'the security of the whole society' are at odds, Smith puts 'security' first.

In May 1773 Smith travelled to London, where he continued working on *The Wealth of Nations* until late 1775, when he sent the manuscript to his publisher. In contrast to his solitary walks on the beach at Kirkcaldy, Smith took advantage of the opportunity to enjoy the much wider range of 'Amusements' that London could offer: reading newspapers and pamphlets in the British Coffeehouse, going to the theatre and public lectures and debating philosophy and current affairs at clubs and dinner parties. Thanks to a standing invitation to attend the dinners of the MP and solicitor-general Alexander Wedderburn, Smith was able to gather insights from those at the heart of government as well as share his own, as yet unpublished views, with policymakers. This activity clearly shaped *The Wealth of Nations*, particularly its closing discussion of what was then the government's most pressing concern: the troubles in the thirteen colonies of North America.

The interests of the colonists and the home nation had been set on divergent courses for some time. The Seven Years War (1756–63), however, had brought these differences into stark relief. Although estimates of the rate of expansion were doubtless inflated, the consensus held that the apparently limitless supply of land and natural resources, combined with high wages, were encouraging a population boom in the American colonies. This encouraged colonists to move ever westwards into the interior, where they clashed both with Native Americans and with the French, who were endeavouring to block this expansion with a series of fortifications along the Mississippi River. This line linked French settlements in Canada and Louisiana. Meanwhile, France's ally Spain (whose king came from the same Bourbon dynasty) claimed Florida.

Ministers in London had sought to avoid conflict with the Bourbon powers by restricting their subjects' westwards expansion. Given the vast distances separating them from the colonial frontier, however, these instructions were widely flouted, and colonial militias created purely for defensive purposes often engaged in low-level skirmishes of a kind that appeared foolhardy to those in London, who well knew that they could find themselves on the hook if this sort of thing got out of hand. Ministers and members of parliament sitting in London would subsequently find themselves having to pay for a war not of their own making. This is effectively what had happened in the 1750s, when a colonial conflict known to

Americans today as the French and Indian War led directly to the outbreak of a worldwide conflict between Britain and the Bourbon powers – that is, to the Seven Years War.

The defeat of the French in the Seven Years' War led to them ceding their Canadian territories to Britain and rolling back the line of fortifications along the Mississippi. All that was left were two small islands in the Gulf of Saint Lawrence, Saint Pierre and Miquelon, and Louisiana. The former are still administered by France; Louisiana and French territory west of the Mississippi were sold by Napoleon to the United States in 1803. Colonists overestimated the degree to which these victories had been won by their own citizen militias, and vastly underestimated the costs to the British state. Britain was left with a greatly expanded national debt that needing servicing. Ministers in London naturally felt that the colonies should share the financial burden with their fellow British subjects living in Britain itself. It was time to draw a line under London's benign neglect of her American colonies, which had been given considerable leeway to manage their own affairs. The imposition of higher customs duties and other revenue-raising initiatives by London might teach the colonists that freedom from the French did not come free. It was, in short, time for the 'mushroom' elite of the colonies (so-called because, in a society where rank was still largely determined by birth, they seemed to have sprung up overnight) to grow up.

The 1765 Stamp Act was the first of these new taxes. It stipulated that all newspapers and any legal contract had to be printed on paper bearing the impress of a stamp (indicating that the paper-maker had paid a special tax; naturally, the papermakers passed this additional charge on to those buying their products). Petitions and protests began, with London initially showing itself willing to compromise, only to become concerned that conciliation might end up encouraging resistance against certain taxes to develop into a coordinated campaign for complete independence. Before the

Carington Bowles (publisher), *A New Method of Macarony Making, as Practised at Boston in North America*, 1774, mezzotint. In Boston and elsewhere, customs officers were tarred and feathered.

Seven Years War the thirteen colonies had been an archipelago; for historical reasons the internal administration and degree of administrative dependence on London differed markedly between, say, Massachusetts (an 'old' colony, conceived as a refuge for a persecuted Protestant sect, with a significant German population) and Georgia (a much 'younger' colony, a penal colony turned tobacco plantation).

The Seven Years War had fostered a more cohesive American identity. A shared British past, ironically enough, provided further means of encouraging resistance. Britain's seventeenth-century history, understood as a heady tale of plucky resistance to the royal 'despotism' of King Charles I, provided a gallery of precedents that could be wheeled in to encourage defiance of the supposed 'despotism' of King George III's ministers – the 'British' governors, customs officials and troops charged with implementing the new taxes and maintaining order in King George's colonies. A few months before Smith's trip to London opponents of a new tax on Indian tea threw an incoming vessel's cargo into Boston harbour. The Boston Tea Party of 1773 led London to take firmer action to maintain its authority, and the colonists to develop an entirely novel complaint of 'no taxation without representation', challenging the authority of the British parliament to take decisions that affected them.

Smith would have been among the many Britons to be deeply puzzled by this mantra, one that seems self-evident to us. Smith himself didn't have the vote, and was not very bothered by that fact. As we have noted, he did not see government as originating in any 'contract'; if theorists like John Locke wrote that Britons were governed by 'consent', then it was at most 'a very figurative metaphoricall consent' (*LJ*, 323). Most Britons felt that parliament was there to represent not mature human beings who happened to have been born in Britain or her colonies, but the landed, manufacturing and trading 'interests' (that is, those who owned the soil and had significant capital invested in factories, ships and so on). Parliament was the heart of Britain's stakeholder democracy: only those with a large stake in the Empire's fortunes (its soil, industry and trade) had a voice. Understood in this sense, America was better represented in the parliament that sat in London than large swathes of England's industrial north were. American 'interests' were represented by those merchants and bankers with large investments in the thirteen colonies, who had entered parliament in the time-honoured fashion: by buying parliamentary seats (either by paying for votes in a certain constituency, or by paying an aristocrat to let them nominate the candidate to one of the parliamentary seats controlled by that aristocrat).

Though the colonists shared a language, history and culture with Britain, the political discourse of liberty and representation the former cobbled together in the 1770s from a mixture of English, Scottish and French ideas was new, and would, as the history of slaveholding indicates, take considerable time to be fully realized. The closing pages of Smith's *Wealth of Nations* would reflect his awareness that Britain's attempt to hold on to her American colonies by force was a waste of time. The best option for London was to give the colonies their independence. That he made the elaboration of this view the climax of his much-awaited treatise would strike some readers as odd – as an indication that he had allowed his stay in London to carry him away from the consideration of a timeless and universal theory of political economy to the consideration of mere affairs of state, matters of momentary interest that would make the book 'too much like a publication for the present moment', as the Edinburgh professor Hugh Blair put it (*c*, 188). Smith seemed to have deprived *The Wealth of Nations* of much of its value and potential impact by advocating what many contemporaries saw as an unrealistic and eccentric policy of unilateral decolonization. It is not as if Smith was a hasty writer; indeed, he seems to have found the process of writing slow and painful, leading him to dictate parts to a secretary rather than write them down himself. How can we explain his decision to end *The Wealth of Nations* in this way?

Smith felt that the costly and bloody war between Britain and her colonies offered a particularly telling illustration of the perils of mercantilism, 'that system or theory which placed the opulence of a nation on its coin and money' (*LJ*, 388). Mercantilists view international trade as a zero-sum game, not as a means by which fellow human beings persuade each other to get what they want. In the mercantilist's vision of the market the seller wins and the buyer loses, and the winner is the country left with the most gold. A mercantilist spirit led all men of business to seek to monopolize their particular trade, and to lobby government to help them reach that goal by enforcing restrictions on production (such as those imposed by guilds) and by using import and export tariffs and bounties (subsidies) to protect them from foreign competition.

Mercantilism led to imperialism because the same mercantilists and statesmen sought to increase national wealth by looking abroad. Fables of an Eldorado or 'City of Gold' suggested that wealth might be accumulated without any economic activity at all, simply by stealing or mining gold and silver (which have no intrinsic value) in Central or South America. As it happens, the Spanish and Portuguese had already made the painful discovery in the sixteenth century that flooding their economies with the New World's gold was in fact harmful, discouraging manufacturing and leading to inflation. For without any domestic production to spend it on or domestic industry in which to invest it, the gold quickly went abroad; largely to rival Protestant states in the north, whose agricultural improvers, manufacturers and traders did have something useful to do with the capital.

While this 'golden dream' of empire had been discredited, the idea of creating an empire of consumers had grown to take its place. The North American colonies were thus restricted from trading with Britain's rival powers and from producing anything other than primary goods that would then be worked up at 'home' in Britain before being sold back to the colonists. Prevented by the monopoly from shopping anywhere else, the colonists would have to buy their finished goods from Britain, who would secure for herself the large margin between the price they paid for colonial materials (indigo, cotton, timber, pig iron) and the price at which they sold the finished goods (dyed cloth, ships, furniture, steel shoe-buckles). 'To found a great empire for the sole purpose of raising up a people of customers,' Smith notes, 'may at first sight appear a project fit only for a nation of shopkeepers.' In fact, it was a project 'altogether unfit for a nation of shopkeepers; but extremely fit for a nation whose government is influenced by shopkeepers' (*WN*, 613).

The final paragraph of *The Wealth of Nations* sees Smith argue that events in North America had demonstrated that, after almost three hundred years of British colonial activity, the mercantilist 'project' had failed. In order to achieve 'the monopoly of the colony trade' the British state had introduced a series of restrictions that had not increased her production, but simply diverted investment from one sector of the economy to a less efficient one, making goods more expensive for the consumer, who also had to pay for armies of soldiers and colonial administrators through increased taxation:

> The rulers of Great Britain have, for more than a century past, amused the people with the imagination that they possessed a great empire on the west side of the Atlantic. This empire, however, has hitherto existed in imagination only. It has hitherto been, not an empire, but the project of an empire; not a gold mine, but the project of a gold mine; a project which has cost, which continues to cost, and which, if pursued in the same way as it has been hitherto, is likely to cost immense expense, without being likely to bring any profit . . . It is surely now time that our rulers should either realize this golden dream, in which they have been indulging themselves, perhaps, as well as the people; or, that they should awake from it themselves, and endeavour to awaken the people. If the project cannot be compleated, it ought to be given up. If any of the provinces of the British empire cannot be made to contribute towards the support of the whole empire, it is surely time that Great Britain should free herself from the expence of defending those provinces in time of war, and of supporting any part of their civil or military

establishments in time of peace, and endeavour to accommodate her future views and designs to the real mediocrity of her circumstances (*wn*, 946–7).

As Smith points out a few pages earlier, an independent United States would continue to trade with Britain, enriching both. Indeed, the new sovereign state and Britain were each other's biggest trade partner well into the following century and beyond. Had Wedderburn and his superiors in the British government taken Smith's advice in 1776, the British state would have been spared five years of war, not only with the colonists but with her formidable rival France (who joined the rebels' side in 1778), a war that burdened both with another vast war debt.

Britain chose to throw away a vast fortune to secure a trade it would have enjoyed (and did eventually enjoy) anyway, had it not gone to war. To give up an empire unilaterally would have been unprecedented, admittedly, and might have come at the cost of Britain's national prestige. When prime minister Lord North told King George III in 1779 that the cost of fighting the colonists bore no relation to any possible gains, His Majesty replied that North was 'only weighing such events in the scale of a tradesman behind his counter'.[4] But the eventual defeat at Yorktown in 1781 would be an equal humiliation. Unable to comprehend that a mighty army of professional troops had been defeated by a ragtag army of backwoodsmen, the British forces marched out of Yorktown to the tune 'The World Turned Upside Down'.

Viewed as an episode in a stadial history of man, mercantilism and the kind of imperialism it fostered seemed to expose a serious flaw in the 'progress of opulence'. Thanks to the creation of consumer luxuries and the resulting decline of feudalism, the average man had become less, rather than more, likely to find himself fighting in a war for his own lord or having his family, neighbourhood or business destroyed by another lord's army.

Unfortunately the merchants and their mercantilism were, it emerged, just as hungry (perhaps more so) to domineer and pursue foolish wars in the expectation that it would enrich them.

> The capricious ambition of kings and ministers has not, during the present and the preceding century, been more fatal to the repose of Europe, than the impertinent jealousy of merchants and manufacturers. The violence and injustice of the rulers of mankind is an ancient evil, for which, I am afraid, the nature of human affairs can scarce admit of a remedy. But the mean rapacity, the monopolizing spirit of merchants and manufacturers, who neither are, nor ought to be the rulers of mankind, though it cannot perhaps be corrected, may very easily be prevented from disturbing the tranquillity of any body but themselves (*wn*, 493).

Smith certainly saw zeal for profit as a risk to public 'tranquillity'. Men of business always paint a picture of their particular branch of trade as one on the verge of collapse, Smith notes, unsettling the public in order to increase the pressure on the state to give them the monopoly they need – for the good of all, supposedly.

Smith's dislike of the tariffs and other restrictions for which men of business successfully lobby is visceral: 'Like the law of Draco,' he observes, 'these laws may be said to be all written in blood' (*wn*, 648). As he had noted in his lectures on jurisprudence in 1762, one regulation intended to boost domestic wool production had seen the exportation of wool made a crime punishable by death (*lj*, 105). Such laws naturally led to smuggling. Rather than describing smugglers as criminals, Smith encourages us to see them as good men criminalized by legislation passed to protect a monopoly. The average smuggler 'would have been, in every respect, an excellent citizen, had not the laws of his country made that a crime which nature never meant to be so' (*wn*, 898). In making his gory simile

Smith was also thinking of the very bloody connections between mercantilism and war. The War of Jenkins's Ear fought between Britain and Spain from 1739 is described as 'a bounty [i.e. subsidy] which has been given in order to support a monopoly'. So was the Seven Years War (*wn*, 616, 615). These men of business were truly as selfish and despotic as the feudal lords had been. Not only did they disturb the public peace, they made trade belligerent, taking the lives of their fellow citizens and burdening the survivors with a share of a massive war debt. Trade – as we have seen, an activity Smith believes is intended by nature to promote international peace and mutual understanding – had itself been prostituted by men of business in a fashion Smith found disgusting.

Sometimes, Smith concedes, these businessmen genuinely believe such measures to be in the public interest, but most of the time it is simply greed. Statesmen are taken in by this rhetoric, partly because they are flattered to imagine themselves able to bring about such prosperity through wise trade policy. Their eminent social position misleads them into thinking that they possess knowledge and intelligence greater than those beneath them, and that they have a duty to direct how the latter invest their money. They could not be more wrong, Smith argues:

> The stateman, who should attempt to direct private people in what manner they ought to employ their capitals, would not only load himself with a most unnecessary attention, but assume an authority which could safely be trusted, not only to no single person, but to no council or senate whatever, and which would nowhere be so dangerous as in the hands of a man who had folly and presumption enough to fancy himself fit to exercise it (*wn*, 456).

It is time to consider Smith's view of government and its duties in more depth.

5

The Machine of Government, 1776–89

The Wealth of Nations was published in two volumes by the
London publisher William Strahan on 9 March 1776. It cost two
pounds and two shillings, approximately £130 in today's prices. In
contrast to *The Theory of Moral Sentiments*, it is clearly structured as
a scientific treatise, with an opening 'Introduction and Plan' as well
as extensive footnotes and an appendix containing figures on the
herring fishing industry (intended to back up Smith's claim that a
bounty or state subsidy had not lowered prices, while encouraging
'rash undertakers' to put to sea 'for the sole purpose of catching,
not the fish, but the bounty'; *wn*, 522, 520). It is organized into five
books. Smith begins by considering the causes of that 'improvement
in the productive powers of labour' witnessed in the transition
from the 'miserably poor', 'savage' nations to 'civilized and thriving
nations' – the specialization of labour taking centre stage. Book two
examines the 'capital stock' of a nation and the different sectors
of the economy in which it could be used to employ 'useful and
productive labourers'. For book three Smith adopts a more
historical approach in analysing the 'progress of opulence'; book
four sees him consider previous 'theories of political economy',
above all 'the mercantile system' (that is, mercantilism). The final
book discusses 'the revenue of the sovereign, or commonwealth',
notably, different forms of taxation and the ends to which that
revenue is put: servicing the national debt, funding defence and
a legal system as well as the provision of education and culture

John Kay, *Lord Rockville, Mr Adam Smith and Commissioner Brown*, 1787, etching with aquatint. Smith (centre) is with the judge Lord Rockville (left) and a fellow Commissioner of Customs.

(*WN*, 10–12). It ends with a plea for Britain to give up her empire. This clear structure is, admittedly, somewhat undermined by a few digressions or tangents, of a sort that Smith presumably felt would be tolerated in a work intended for statesmen and philosophers, rather than students.

And the statesmen and philosophers were duly impressed by what was in effect the first sustained work of 'political oeconomy', a field Smith himself described as 'a branch of the science of a statesman or legislator' (*WN*, 428). 'You have formed into a regular and consistent system one of the most intricate and important parts of political science', the Scottish historian William Robertson wrote, venturing to hope that *The Wealth of Nations* 'will occasion a total change in several important articles both in police [policy] and finance' (*c*, 192). Equally impressed, Hume noted that the work was 'probably much improved by your last Abode in London' and looked forward to Smith returning to Scotland so that he could debate certain points with him (*c*, 186). Unfortunately it was evident from his severe weight loss that Hume was suffering from a form of cancer, of which he died on 25 August 1776. Instead of discussing questions of rent and coinage, Hume and Smith's final exchanges were focused on Hume's plans for his literary estate.

In addition to a new edition of his work, Hume wanted an autobiographical fragment (*My Own Life*) to be published, along with an early work entitled *Dialogues Concerning Natural Religion*, which he had circulated in manuscript form back in 1750. This work attacked natural theology, that is, the science by which one gleans an understanding of God, the Creator from the study of Creation and the principles that apparently underpin its design. Smith asked Hume to leave him discretion not to publish them (as it happens, Hume gave another copy to his nephew, who had Strahan publish the *Dialogues* anonymously in 1779). Though Smith's decision might seem somewhat shuffling towards his great friend, there is no doubting the feeling with which Smith described Hume's death, in a letter published together with Hume's *My Own Life* in 1777. Smith's description of Hume 'as approaching as nearly to the idea of a perfectly wise and virtuous man, as perhaps the nature of human frailty will permit' was strong meat to Scottish churchmen, who portrayed atheists as the blackest form of sinner and who were wont to depict the 'scoffer's' deathbed in much more lurid colours (*c*, 221).

Upon his return to Kirkcaldy in 1777 Smith had begun a work on aesthetics, coming back to a subject he had addressed in his Edinburgh lectures of 1749. Smith was particularly interested in the role played by imitation in music and dance. Although this work would never be published, perishing in the flames after Smith's death, Smith's Edinburgh lectures and two papers presented to the Glasgow Literary Society in 1788 are nonetheless striking as early attempts to argue that music was not in fact imitative (that is, built around vocal music's resemblance to bird song, say), but gave an intellectual pleasure on account of its systematic arrangement of sounds. Our pleasure was a harmless result of our 'love of system'.

This and other planned works might have come to fruition had Smith not served as one of the five commissioners who sat on the Board of Customs in Edinburgh. Although the success of *The Wealth of Nations* doubtless played a part, lobbying by Buccleuch lay behind this appointment in 1778, which came with a salary of £600 (£38,000 today). With his characteristic eye for probity, Smith offered to give up the pension he received from Buccleuch, who refused. Smith moved from Kirkcaldy to Canongate in Edinburgh. His household now included, in addition to his elderly mother and cousin, nine-year-old David Douglas, Smith's cousin and designated heir. The Board of Customs met four days a week and required Smith to master a raft of customs legislation. This legislation was the product of decades of mercantilist tinkering with tariffs, bounties and other wheezes intended to boost the Scottish economy while 'beggaring all their neighbours' (*WN*, 493).

In an age where it was very hard to come at economic statistics of any kind, a commissionership had a certain appeal to someone curious about political economy. As a customs official Smith enjoyed wide-ranging powers to investigate economic activity of all kinds. He presumably used this access to refine later editions of *The Wealth of Nations*. The irony of Smith being responsible for implementing mercantilist regulations was evident from his very first day in office.

He later wrote to the MP and First Lord of the Board of Trade William Eden of his surprise at arriving at Custom House in Edinburgh's Royal Exchange Square for his first day of work and being confronted with a large board listing all the contraband it was the board's duty to hunt out and destroy. Smith described his surprise at finding 'that I had scarce a stock, a cravat, a pair of ruffles, or a pocket hankerchief which was not prohibited to be worn or used in Great Britain'. 'I wished to set an example,' he continued, 'and burnt them all', cheekily adding that he advised Eden against examining 'either your own or Mrs Edens apparel or household furniture, least you be brought into a scrape of the same kind'. Though intended as a humorous dig, Smith could not help but point to the lesson that such mercantilist prohibitions always failed to produce the intended effects; that is, to boost domestic production and stop foreign manufacturers from producing for the British market. As the contents of Smith's wardrobe demonstrated, prohibited goods still entered the country, albeit as contraband carried by smugglers, on which Customs collected no dues. 'The sole effect of a prohibition is to hinder the revenue from profiting by the importation' (c, 245–6). Prosecuting the smugglers must have been a particularly unpleasant duty for the new commissioner, considering Smith's views of them as victims criminalized by legislation that itself offended against 'natural justice'.

Smith attended board meetings assiduously, far more assiduously than he needed to, or than his admirers had expected him to. Former students were frustrated to see Smith's time taken up with administrative work they considered far less important than his writing. They had expected him to treat the commissionership the way his friend Hume had treated the post of Librarian to the Advocates' Library in Edinburgh, to which he was appointed in 1752 – that is, as a sinecure, an opportunity to spend his time on more congenial and intellectual pursuits. But if Smith had a model in mind, it was not his friend Hume but his neighbour Lord Kames. While Hume had considered settling down among the *philosophes* of Paris and disdained to turn his intellectual powers to anything as grubby as peat and fertilizer, Kames never left Scotland and combined a legal career with service to Scottish philosophy, jurisprudence, literature, agriculture and manufacturing. By this point, admittedly, Kames was very old. On 12 December 1782 he made his last appearance in Scotland's Court of Session. As his fellow judges patted him on the back Kames made his fond goodbyes: 'Fare ye a'weel, ye bitches.' Fifteen days later, he was dead.

Two years later, Smith suffered a much heavier loss: that of his mother, Margaret. As he wrote to his publisher, William Strahan:

> Tho' the death of a person in the ninetieth year of her
> age was no doubt an event most agreable to the course of
> nature; and, therefore, to be foreseen and prepared for;
> yet I must say to you, what I have said to other people, that
> the final separation from a person who certainly loved me
> more than any other person ever did or ever will love me;
> and whom I certainly loved and respected more than I ever
> shall either love or respect any other person, I cannot help
> feeling, even at this hour, as a very heavy stroke upon me . . .
> My friends grow very thin in the world, and I do not find
> that my new ones are likely to supply their place (c, 275).

Smith began to ponder how much time he himself had left. In a letter written the following year to his French friend the Duc de La Rochefoucauld, Smith blamed his slow progress on his 'two other great works', not on the customs house, but on 'the indolence of old age'. 'Tho' I struggle violently against it', Smith wrote, he felt it 'coming fast upon me'. He did not hold out much hope of completing them, either the 'Philosophical History of all the different branches of Literature, of Philosophy, Poetry and Eloquence' or the 'theory and History of Law and Government'. Though 'the materials of both are in a great measure collected', he couldn't seem to work them up (*c*, 286–7). Whatever the cause, Smith's priority in the 1780s lay not in rushing out new work, but in ensuring that he was happy with the form in which he would leave *The Theory of Moral Sentiments* and *The Wealth of Nations*.

To that end Smith secured two leaves of absence that allowed him to travel down to London in 1782 and 1787, where he could be closer to his publishers. His second trip also allowed him to be operated on by the eminent surgeon Sir William Hunter, either for haemorrhoids or an obstruction in his intestine. In London Smith once again socialized with members of the political elite, including important figures in William Pitt's government. Though these men admired Smith's work and even cited it in support of a 1786 free trade treaty with France (named after the aforementioned William Eden), they do not appear to have made much of the opportunity to pick Smith's brain on policy questions.

How did Smith perceive this science and the relationship between 'the people' and the law-makers, the legislators? What was the relationship between a 'public-spirited' desire to promote the public good and the actual 'progress of opulence', which had emancipated western Europe from feudal dependence? To answer these questions we need to draw not only on *The Theory of Moral Sentiments* and *The Wealth of Nations* but on the 1760s lectures on jurisprudence, which presumably constituted the 'materials' Smith planned to work up for his 'theory and History of Law and Government'. Unfortunately Smith burned the text of these lectures, and so we have to rely on two sets of student transcriptions redis- covered in 1895 and 1958 respectively: the so-called 'Report of 1762–3' (six bound volumes) and the 'Report dated 1766' (a single volume, that probably dates from 1763–4). The transcribers likely tidied up and partially reconstructed these texts from shorthand notes taken in Smith's lectures. The 'Report dated 1766' may have been prepared with a view to sale to another student, as a kind of crib. Obviously we cannot be sure of their accuracy. Few professors would be comfortable in the knowledge that posterity's only source for their ideas lay in their undergraduate students' notes.

In the same way that Smith feels that reading Hutcheson's treatise on benevolence and the moral sense leads Hutcheson's readers to act in a public-spirited way, so he states in *The Theory of Moral Sentiments* that:

> Nothing tends so much to promote public spirit as the study of politics, of the several systems of civil government, their advantages and disadvantages, of the constitution of our own country, its situation, and interest with regard to foreign nations, its commerce, its defence, the disadvantages it labours under, the dangers to which it may be exposed, how to remove the one, and how to guard against the other. Upon this account political disquisitions, if just, and reasonable, are of all works of speculation the most useful.

Contemplating Hutcheson's system of moral philosophy makes us feel good about our own potential to act virtuously and may indeed result in 'right' behaviour. But this does not mean that this system, built around a supposed moral sense, actually offers a coherent account of why we call certain actions 'right' and certain ones 'wrong'. As we have seen, Smith shows us how Hutcheson's system does not offer such an explanation. Contemplating the 'connexions and dependencies' of a particular 'system of civil government' (the famous 'checks and balances' of the United States constitution, drafted in 1787, for example) makes us feel good about ourselves and can 'implant public virtue in the breast of him who seems heedless of the interest of his country' (*TMS*, 186). But that does not mean that those 'connexions and dependencies' actually offer a coherent account of why we call certain 'systems of civil government' just and certain ones unjust.

Seen in this light, the 'science of politics' and 'political economy' are means of persuasion, means of rousing virtuous feelings that will, once unleashed, do the actual 'work' of making human society better. These feelings are founded on 'the beauty of utility', that is, on aesthetics. They are directed not at real utility, but at the appearance of utility. This seems a roundabout route to good government. If, as Smith says, the 'sole use and end' of 'all constitutions of government' is 'the happiness of those who live under them', why aren't we led to perfect those constitutions simply out of a desire to promote that happiness? This is because we are often misled by a taste for 'system', 'a certain love of art and contrivance'.

Smith argues that far from being restricted to questions of government, our tendency to prefer the appearance of utility over real utilility can be illustrated 'in a thousand instances'. Anyone who has ever shared a house with a fastidiously neat person knows that they can exhibit a strong preference for furniture to be arranged in a certain way, even if it isn't convenient. In Smith's day chairs and tables normally stood against the walls of a room whenever the room was not in use, being brought forward and arranged as required, before being replaced. Smith imagines a scenario in which someone might inconvenience himself by moving such furniture around, precisely because he wishes the appearance of convenience:

When a person comes into his chamber, and finds the chairs all standing in the middle of the room, he is angry with his servant, and rather than see them continue in that disorder, perhaps takes the trouble himself to set them all in their places with their backs to wall. The whole propriety of this new situation arises from its superior conveniency in leaving the floor free and disengaged. To attain this conveniency he voluntarily puts himself to more trouble than all he could have suffered from the want of it; since nothing was more easy, than to have set himself down upon one of them [the chairs], which is probably what he does when his labour is over (*TMS*, 180).

If real utility was the basis of all beauty and virtue, Smith notes, we would have 'no other reason for praising a man than that for which we commend a chest of drawers' (*TMS*, 188). Clearly the fact that the man has passions which we can share (or not), while the chest of drawers does not, leads us to feel differently about them. Smith takes a certain pride in this observation, which, he writes, 'has not, so far as I know, been yet taken notice of by any body' (*TMS*, 180). As he hints on the previous page, it represented a hole in the arguments of Hume. Though not named, Smith clearly has Hume in mind when referring to 'an ingenious and agreeable philosopher' who argues that we admire an object's utility because it suggests 'the pleasure or conveniency which it is fitted to promote'.

To return to Smith's target, the man 'who seems heedless of the interest of his country', we will not rouse him to act for 'public virtue' by describing to him the material benefits that 'the subjects of a well-governed state' enjoy. We do not appeal to his benevolence. Instead, we do so by referring to how the 'several wheels of the machine of government [might] be made to move with more harmony and smoothness, without grating upon one another, or mutually retarding one another's motions' (*TMS*, 186). We appeal to his 'love of contrivance', to the pleasure he takes in observing a well-oiled and engineered machine. Why is this? Why does the interest we take in questions of political economy and constitutions differ from the interest Smith says we all naturally take in the fortunes of others? Why is it that such discussion renders us 'eager to promote the happiness of our fellow-creatures, rather from a view to perfect and improve a certain beautiful and orderly system, than from any immediate sense or feeling of what they either suffer or enjoy' (*TMS*, 185)?

This is because 'humanity' and 'public spirit', though allied qualities, make very different demands of us. To be humane all we need to do is perform 'what this exquisite sympathy would of its own accord prompt us to do' (in the manner described in Chapter Two). To show public spirit, however, we must place another person's interests and feelings above our own. When I cease to pursue a promotion at work because I imagine 'that the services of another are better entitled to it', Smith points out, I am not acting out of sympathy with the other person's sentiment of joy. The only way that sympathy could lead me to act in this way would be if I somehow imagined that the joy felt by that other person on being promoted was greater than the joy I would feel myself, were I to get the promotion instead of her. I do not, in other words, pull back because 'I feel more exquisitely what concerns that other person than what concerns [myself]'. That would be impossible; after all, my first duty is to take care of myself, and I cannot feel the same 'pitch' of joy as the person directly affected can. No, I act in this manner because I view the bigger picture: 'by an effort of magnanimity' I act according to the 'view of things' that I feel 'must naturally occur to any third person'. Instead of feeling miserable, I feel the approval of an Impartial Spectator. Whether or not I actually receive this praise, I have the pleasing consciousness of merit, of being praiseworthy. The 'sentiment of approbation arises from the perception of this beauty of utility', Smith concludes, 'it has no reference of any kind to the sentiments of others' (TMS, 191, 192).

The beauty of systems lies in the fact that, like a well-made watch, their 'connexions and dependencies' make up a complicated network of different elements that function only if they are put together in a particular arrangement.

> The wheels of the watch are all admirably adjusted to the end
> for which it was made, the pointing of the hour. All their
> various motions conspire in the nicest manner to produce
> this effect. If they were endowed with a desire and intention

to produce it, they could not do it better. Yet we never ascribe any such desire or intention to them, but to the watch-maker, and we know that they are put into motion by a spring, which intends the effect it produces as little as they do (*TMS*, 87).

In such machines we distinguish between 'efficient' and 'final' causes. Unfortunately, however, when 'nature' and 'reason' lead us in a parallel direction we give the credit to the latter (the final cause) rather than the former (the efficient cause).

'When by natural principles we are led to advance those ends, which a refined and enlightened reason would recommend to us', we ignore the 'natural principles' and instead claim that we are moved to admire those who are public-spirited (and punish those who are not) by 'universal benevolence', 'the necessity of justice', 'the beauty of utility' or 'public virtue' (or, we might add, 'democratic principles', indeed) (*TMS*, 87). Yet these are all second-order, intellectual rationalizations, Smith insists, something very different from the 'natural principles' that in fact lead us to act. As the historian Knud Haakonssen notes, with Smith we must distinguish between

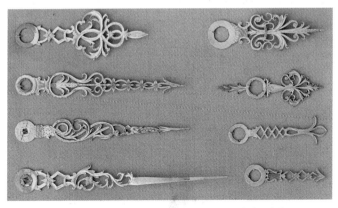

'If they were endowed with a desire and intention' of 'pointing the hour', these eighteenth-century French clock hands 'could not do it better'. But we know they have no such 'desire'.

'the reasons that justify and motives that lead, and the order of things that ensues'.[1] First we are led to act by our natural instincts; only afterwards do we try to justify why we acted in terms of these principles.

As we have seen, mercantilists were constantly urging the statesman to intervene in the name of the public good. So, too, were the Physiocrats and other 'men of system', who looked to the statesman to impose radical reforms from above. In *The Wealth of Nations* Smith names Quesnay, attributing to him the view that 'the political body' could thrive only 'under a certain precise regimen'. The only scenario in which France could thrive, therefore, was if Quesnay's Physiocratic programme was implemented in full, with all its 'connexions and dependencies,' and without any regard to the individuals affected. Quesnay's programme had failed to acknowledge 'the natural effort which every man is continually making to better his own condition', a 'principle of preservation' by which that political body could prosper despite 'the bad effects of a political oeconomy, in some degree, both partial and oppressive'. 'If a nation could not prosper without the enjoyment of perfect liberty and perfect justice, there is not in the world a nation which could ever have prospered' (*WN*, 674). Elsewhere Smith goes further, noting that 'mere justice' (that is, pure justice) is 'upon most occasions, but a negative virtue'. It is mainly about telling us what not to do. 'We may often fulfil all the rules of justice by sitting still and doing nothing' (*TMS*, 82).

Smith's faith that our innate dispositions will not only preserve society, but allow it to enjoy a measure of prosperity regardless of the particular system of political economy, or indeed the particular form of government espoused by those in authority, is probably intended to be reassuring. Whether the statesman sits still or adopts measures in obedience to this or that system of 'political oeconomy', the outcome will be more or less the same: greater prosperity for all. Yet to us today there are several ways in which this seems unsatisfying. Acknowledging the power of instinct over us and over our destiny feels tantamount to a surrender of our right to self-determination. Recognition of this right is both just and a precious inheritance, it is something we feel ourselves to enjoy as beneficiaries of a historical struggle for the vote, freedom of conscience, free speech and so on. It feels both irresponsible and ungrateful not to cherish these things. We cannot, it seems, help but feel that human society should be governed by 'written and formall laws', even if a glance at human history is enough to make us concede the accuracy of Smith's claim that such laws in fact represent 'a very great refinement of government . . . such as we never meet but in the latest periods of it' (*LJ*, 213). It is more flattering to our individual dignity, certainly, to believe that we inhabit a well-ordered 'machine of government', and that we consent to be taxed and to perform the other duties that the state imposes on us.

It was to be expected, Smith admits, that experience of how certain actions tend to elicit pleasant sentiments and others unpleasant ones would lead us to form 'general rules which determined what actions are, and what are not, the objects of each of those sentiments' – that is, a morality. Once established, however, we could find ourselves appealing to these rules 'as the ultimate foundations of what is just and unjust in human conduct'. They can if necessary supply a standard of 'duty' sufficient in itself to operate as 'the only principle', 'directing their actions' even without a moral sense based on propriety. 'There is scarce any man, however, who by discipline, education, and example, may not', Smith states, 'be so impressed with a regard to general rules, as to act upon almost every occasion with tolerable decency, and through the whole of his life to avoid any considerable degree of blame' (*TMS*, 162–3). Smith's emphasis on fostering individual moral judgement rather than laying down a set of rules, however, makes this seem second-best. At the other end of the social spectrum the same eye for 'rules' mislead 'several very eminent authors' into imagining that our judgements of right and wrong 'were formed like the decisions of a court of judicatory, by considering first the general rule, and then, secondly, whether the particular action under consideration fell properly within its comprehension' (*TMS*, 160). While the demands of 'mere justice' (founded on resentment) can be considered in this way, those of benevolence (such as gratitude) cannot. What court could or would enforce us to perform the duty of gratitude? Enforced charity is not generosity – beneficence must be 'free' to be beneficence.

'Government was established to defend the property of the subjects', Smith states (*LJ*, 324). Paying taxes enables us to enjoy the greater tranquillity and security, both for our bodies and possessions, that comes with good government. 'Eminent authors' understood this in terms of a contract between sovereign and subject. According to this widespread view, if our legislators do not provide that tranquillity and security, we can resist them. Smith insists that our allegiance is not based on a voluntary contract, whether explicit or tacit. Even if it were, this would not be a just order.

> The foundation of the allegiance of the people being a tacit contract is not at all just, and we see accordingly that few of those limitations laid down by writers who follow that scheme are to be found in fact in any country . . . It is a rule laid down by Mr. Locke as a principle that the people have a right to resist whenever the sovereign takes their money from them without their consent by levying taxes to which they have not agreed. Now we see that in France, Spain, etc. the consent of the people is not in the least thought of; the king imposes what taxes he pleases. It is in Britain alone that any consent of the people is required, and God knows it is but a very figurative metaphoricall consent which is given here. And in Scotland still more than in

England, as but very few have a vote for a Member of Parliament who give this metaphoricall consent; and yet this is not any where reckoned a sufficient cause of rebellion (*LJ*, 323–4).

Only 'a very small part of the people, such as have read Locke' speak of such consent (*LJ*, 316). Smith points out that both the justice and democracy some of us like to talk about are 'metaphoricall', an exercise in 'as-if'. As with the Physiocrats, we are warned against taking the pretty models for reality.

Perhaps the greatest problem we have with Smith is this apparent neglect of or sneering at politics. Whether as a historian or as a psychologist explaining our motivations, Smith puts last what we think should come first. He puts security and prosperity before justice and freedom. *Fiat justitia, ruat caelum* (Let justice be done, though the heavens may fall). We might well utter the same imprecation with regard to *libertas* (freedom). We can value these things for their own sake, not as a means to another end or as the unintended side-effects of that end. Yet this is all Smith seems to be offering. For him, the tyranny of the feudal lords ended, setting their army of retainers free from arbitrary rule and dependence, not as the direct result of retainers claiming their 'natural rights' but as an unintended consequence of the lords' newfound ability to indulge their unfathomable vanity in 'trinkets of frivolous utility'. The resulting 'progress of opulence' eventually brought us (again by a somewhat roundabout route) to a state 'where the necessaries and conveniencies of life are easily come at'. 'Nothing else can deserve the name of opulence but this comeattibleness' (*LJ*, 343). Even the word seems unsatisfyingly clunky.

If we do not consent to do so in some sort of exchange, why else do we obey the authorities? Smith's answer is that we rarely stop to think about such things. Obedience is unthinking. The obedience of the majority, Smith says, is based on a 'principle of authority', a respect of and deference to those in authority similar to the respect we bear our own parents. It is also based on a 'principall of common or generall interest', a slightly more thoughtful deference based on a sense that it is more advisable to submit to the established government than subvert it (*LJ*, 318). Though the administration of justice under it be 'not in the most perfect manner' and though 'there are inconveniences in the government', we recognize that trying to 'subvert' the government 'when it acts with ordinary moderation and tollerable decency' is to risk losing our lives and property in the ensuing unrest and confusion (*LJ*, 322). Smith is willing to concede that subjects are entitled to resist when faced with 'a gross, flagran[t] and palpable abuse' of power, but does not see the point of trying to identify the precise point at which resistance becomes justified. No such fixed point exists, as far as he is concerned; it will vary from case to case.

The first duty of government is to defend its subjects from the attack of another state. Defence in some cases trumps those subjects' freedom and Smith's hatred of state-enforced monopoly. First introduced in 1651, the Navigation Acts were intended to secure Britain's naval defences by ensuring that she would always have a large pool of experienced sailors to man her ships. These Acts required that goods be carried between Britain and her colonies only in 'British bottoms', that is, British merchant vessels manned with British sailors. Smith lived at a time when Britain frequently found herself at war with France and other European powers. At such times rapid mobilization was very important. Though Smith noted that the Navigation Acts were a major bar to foreign participation in international trade with Britain, the defence of the country depended on the 'number of its sailors and shipping'. Thus the Acts 'very properly [endeavour] to give the sailors and shipping of Great Britain the monopoly of the trade in their own country' (*WN*, 463).

There was much debate in Smith's time over whether Britain's land forces should consist of a professional army (who could be mercenaries hired from one of the poorer German states, such as those employed to fight the rebel colonists in North America) paid for by central government or a militia made up of citizen soldiers who fought, not for pay, but to defend their own country. Buccleuch's Fencibles were an example of this kind of volunteer force, strongly admired by Smith's friend Adam Ferguson. Similar ad hoc volunteer forces sprang up in Edinburgh in 1745, ostensibly to protect the city against the Jacobite forces under Bonnie Prince Charlie. They proved to be worthless. Although Smith was in Oxford at the time, the 'Forty-five' nonetheless offered a striking spectacle: a bunch of ill-educated, poor, axe-wielding Highland peasants marched unopposed across populated, wealthy and 'developed' areas of Scotland – and continued south into England.

Smith seems to be pulled both ways on this question. On the one hand he is aware that the invention of gunpowder and firearms have made war a straightforward question of capital rather than one of manpower or even patriotism: the state that has more capital wins because it can afford more guns, powder and bullets than its rival. In modern warfare death is dealt from a distance, by one group of men to another group of men, rather than in battles consisting of a series of face-to-face duels of strength. High levels of training, equipment and discipline are much more necessary thanks to 'the invisible death to which every man feels himself every moment exposed . . . a long time before the battle can be well said to be engaged' (*WN*, 699). This makes war not only 'a very intricate and complicated science', but effectively a 'trade' in itself (*WN*, 695). The invention of gunpowder had the unintended benefit of protecting commercial states from the armies of pastoral or agricultural states to which they had previously been exposed. The variety and seasonal nature of the agricultural way of life made an agricultural population not only physically stronger, but free to head off on campaign in the summer, when there isn't much to do on the farm, without losing output. In a commercial society labour is not only much more specialized (fewer workers are kept in all-round physical

Matthew Darly after Edward Topham, *A March of the Train Bands*, 1777, etching.
A militia might foster community feeling, but was no use in modern war.

fitness) but continuous; though the crops keep growing whether
the farmer is on the farm or the battlefield, non-agricultural
production ceases the moment the pin-maker joins the army.

On the other hand, Smith can see how the kind of weekend
soldiering associated with reserve or militia forces encourages fellow-
feeling of a patriotic kind. A community that exercises together will
not only enjoy better health (a good in itself) but will be happier,
as those of different trades and ranks who are thrown together
will develop 'habitual affection' by sympathizing with each other.
As we know, even if the passions being sympathetically shared by
such people are unpleasant (discomfort at sleeping out in a wet
field, disgust at eating poor food, irritation at regulations that have
only the appearance of utility, and so on), the very act of sharing
emotions brings pleasure. Smith seems to lean towards seeing these
things as so worthwhile as to outweigh the fact that such soldiers
will be less effective as a military force than full-time mercenaries.
'Even though the martial spirit of the people were of no use towards
the defence of society', he argues, such exercises might well serve the

'publick good' (*wn*, 787–8). It seems fair to assume that Smith would have supported a system of enforced national service.

Government also has a duty to educate its subjects. As with Smith's views of a militia, so here there is a sense in which Smith's government is trying to compensate for the harmful effects of the specialization of labour on labourers. The idea that the subdivision of labour led to the so-called 'alienation', or 'estrangement', of the workers would lie at the heart of Karl Marx's criticism of what he called capitalism. In the *Economic and Philosophic Manuscripts of 1844* Marx argues that because the working man does not own what he produces and is, in fact, 'coerced' into making it, the produce of his labour confronts him as 'something hostile and alien'.[2] Smith's account of this effect is painted in lurid colours:

> The man whose whole life is spent in performing a few simple operations, of which the effects too are, perhaps, always the same, or very nearly the same, has no occasion to exert his understanding, or to exercise his invention in finding out expedients for removing difficulties which never occur. He naturally loses, therefore, the habit of such exertion, and generally becomes as stupid and ignorant as it is possible for a human creature to become. The torpor of his mind renders him, not only incapable of relishing or bearing a part in any rational conversation, but of conceiving any generous, noble, or tender sentiment, and consequently of forming any just judgment concerning many even of the ordinary duties of private life . . . The uniformity of his stationary life naturally corrupts the courage of his mind . . . corrupts even the activity of his body, and renders him incapable of exerting his strength with vigour and perseverance . . . His dexterity at his own particular trade seems, in this manner, to be acquired at the expense of his intellectual, social, and martial virtues. But in every improved and civilized society this is the state into which

the labouring poor, that is, the great body of the people, must necessarily fall, unless government takes some pains to prevent it (*WN*, 781–2).

'Dexterity' here seems to result in 'deformity', as the language Smith uses to describe this state equates it to severe physical handicap: 'He is as much mutilated and deformed in his mind', Smith writes, 'as another is in his body, who is either deprived of some of its most essential members, or has lost the use of them.' If anything, the worker was in an even worse position, 'because happiness and misery, which reside altogether in the mind, must necessarily depend more upon the healthful or unhealthful, the mutilated or entire state of the mind, than upon that of the body' (*WN*, 787).

But Smith does not stop there. He goes on to describe the serious political risks incurred. Far from their weakened physical state and 'torpor' transforming them into drones posing no danger to the government, the workers' inability to think straight leaves them prone to being duped by demagogues. Their critical faculties dulled, they are unable to see through revolutionary schemes that promise them Utopia. They will be prone 'to the delusions of enthusiasm or superstition, which, among ignorant nations, frequently occasion the most dreadful disorders' (*WN*, 788). Although we may immediately think of political 'projectors' here (and Smith would probably consider the communist Marx such a one), this line is probably intended to refer to religious 'enthusiasm' (that is, fanaticism) as well.

Smith says that we can combat this dangerous 'torpor' through state-funded provision of 'diversions' intended to keep the people from becoming too melancholy. These could be seen as 'bread and circuses' in a case of 'all work and no play . . .'. What exactly Smith means here is unclear, but he may have meant state-supported music and theatre. While in Paris Smith himself certainly enjoyed attending performances of the French opera – a state-funded cultural initiative. Although he himself does not appear to have danced, he did think and write about dancing, and so perhaps we might include that, too. He clearly does not see state funding for the arts as wasteful.

Smith spends more time discussing the second solution: state-sponsored education. In practice, he says, this will primarily be education of the poor. This is not simply because the poor are less likely than the wealthy to be able to pay for the education of their own children. It is because the poor will be under pressure to put their children to work earlier, in order to supplement household income. Standards in education will, Smith says, differ.

> But though the common people cannot, in any civilized
> society, be so well instructed as people of some rank and
> fortune, the most essential parts of education, however, to
> read, write, and account, can be acquired at so early a period
> of life, that the greater part even of those who are to be bred
> to the lowest occupations, have time to acquire them before
> they can be employed in those occupations. For a very small
> expence the publick can facilitate, can encourage, and can
> even impose upon almost the whole body of the people, the
> necessity of acquiring those most essential parts of education.

The 'publick' should set up a schoolhouse in every parish and pay part (but not all) of the teacher's salary (*wn*, 785). Drawing on the experience of his Oxford years, Smith is concerned that if teachers or university lecturers are paid entirely by the state or by income from an endowment they will fail to attend to their duties. Though poor parents may pay only a small sum, by paying something (rather than not paying at all) they provide an incentive for the teacher to do their job.

Smith's views on the state's duty to provide a free, fair, accessible and impartial legal system are unremarkable, and round off his account of the state's responsibilities. He then turns to consider the revenues of the state, such as taxation. Taxes should weigh more heavily on the rich than the poor, but should not require invasions of privacy. Smith sees having to declare one's income as such an invasion, so he presumably would have opposed the introduction of the income tax by prime minister William Pitt in 1797. Instead Smith prefers taxes on consumption, particularly taxes on luxuries, where the consumption is a matter of choice. Those driving large 'carriages of luxury', for example, should pay more in road tax than drivers of wagons and coaches (*wn*, 725). Smith may have advocated such taxes on moral grounds, as a curb on 'the indolence and vanity of the rich'.

Otherwise Smith advocates an end to bounties and moderate duties on imports and exports: 'High taxes, sometimes by diminishing the consumption of the taxed commodities, and sometimes by encouraging smuggling, frequently afford a smaller revenue to government than what might be drawn from more moderate taxes' (*wn*, 884). He does, admittedly, come close to advocating a bounty to fund the transport of coal to those regions where it is not in abundance, seeing it as unfair on the poor that the tax on 'sea coal' (coal carried down from the coal-rich north of England to the south in barges) makes this fuel even more expensive than it need otherwise be (*wn*, 874). Given his emphasis on tranquillity, it is hardly surprising that he emphasizes the need for the amount, time and manner of paying taxes to be clear to all. The history of all nations demonstrates that even 'a very small degree of uncertainty' is a worse evil than even 'a very considerable degree of inequality' (*wn*, 826).

Conclusion:
Head, Heart and Hand, 1790

Despite enjoying first-rate medical treatment for his intestinal problems during his visits to London in 1782 and 1787, Smith's health did not improve. This, combined with the aforementioned 'indolence of old age', led him to prioritize. Where other writers might have chosen to rush new works into print, Smith put his draft works on law and government to one side and instead devoted his time and energies to revising his first book for a new edition. There had been four English editions published since *The Theory of Moral Sentiments* first appeared in 1759, as well as one German and two French translations. Smith knew this sixth edition would be the last one prepared by the author. In the 'Advertisement' Smith explains that 'the different accidents of my life' had hitherto prevented him from revising *The Theory of Moral Sentiments* as carefully as he intended. Since 1759, he noted, 'several corrections, and a good many illustrations of the doctrines contained in it, have occurred to me' (*TMS*, 3).

Smith added a new section (Part VI), fitted in between Part V, considering the effects of fashion on our moral judgements, and the more historical survey of other systems of moral philosophy in Part VII. The added force given to the description of fashion's harmful influence in Part V and the emphasis on 'prudence' in the new Part VI could be seen as a case of Smith trying to apply various patches to lessen the contrast between *The Theory of Moral Sentiments* and *The Wealth of Nations*. By his own account Smith's new Part VI constituted 'a practical system of Morality, under the title of the

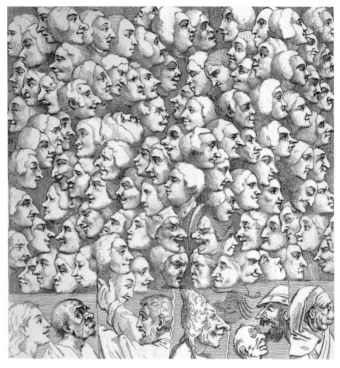

William Hogarth, *Characters and Caricaturas*, 1743, etching.

Character of Virtue' (*c*, 320). This statement suggests that 'the different accidents of my life' and writing *The Wealth of Nations* had not led Smith to lower his sights from a self and a society motivated by a love of virtue to one that sought to satisfy a businesslike prudence. As we shall see, Smith certainly did see a society built on 'cold prudence' as possessing a good deal of prosperity and tranquillity. But it was second-best. Alongside 'cold prudence' was a 'superior prudence' that had more to offer.

The new edition of *The Theory of Moral Sentiments* appeared in June 1790. Since at least January 1790 a shaking in his hand had been making it hard for Smith to write, while his illness prevented him from attending the customs house or paying social calls. In one of his final letters Smith wrote to his London publisher, Thomas Cadell, asking how the new edition was selling: 'You may safely tell me the truth as I am grown almost perfectly indifferent both as to praise and as to abuse' (*c*, 324). Unlike the Poor Man's Son, Smith kept on enjoying mental, if not physical, tranquillity right up to 17 July 1790, when he died at his Edinburgh home, Panmure House. He was buried five days later in the churchyard of Canongate.

His death was hardly noted in the press. As Hume's friend, Smith had been embarrassed by the opulence of Hume's elaborate mausoleum, which stands proudly on Calton Hill in Edinburgh. Smith's own grave was marked by a much simpler stone in the city below, and today is easily overlooked. Unlike Hume, Smith did not put in place elaborate measures to ensure that unpublished manuscripts were seen through the press. Smith initially planned to leave instructions for his executors to burn everything except a manuscript, 'History of Astronomy', which they published in 1790. Near his end, fearing that these instructions might not be followed, he incinerated sixteen volumes of material himself. Smith did not devote any time to penning autobiographical musings like Rousseau's vast *Confessions* or Hume's shorter *My Own Life*.

Here again Smith practised what he preached. As he put it in *The Theory of Moral Sentiments*, 'Though every man may, according to the proverb, be the whole world to himself, to the rest of mankind he is a most insignificant part of it' (*TMS*, 83). Quite apart from holding such musings to be unlikely to interest readers, Smith's belief in the fundamental equality of human beings would also have discouraged him. Autobiography tends to present a human being's achievements as destiny, rather than a series of 'different accidents'; as the inevitable product of innate character traits and a unique personality. For Smith, by contrast, the philosopher and the 'porter' are indistinguishable at birth, their different 'destinies' the result of 'habit, custom and education' (*WN*, 29). Unfortunately, consumer society encourages us to view ourselves as uniquely significant, by promising us that among the dizzying variety on offer there is, somewhere, a product that is 'right for me', that expresses 'my individuality'. Social media offers further opportunities to stoke this 'curated self'. It is unsurprising that we therefore consider these selves more and more fascinatingly unique than was common in Smith's day, even as our choices become more predictable and less unique. A survey of American teenagers held in 2005 found that 80 per cent considered themselves 'very important'. The figure for 1950 was 12 per cent. Meanwhile the 'median narcissism score' produced by asking a similar cohort if they agree with a series of statements (including 'somebody should write a biography about me') has risen 30 per cent in the past twenty years.[1] A thinker and observer as acute and as modest as Adam Smith, one who recognized that any 'self' was not born, but made by fellow human beings, was unlikely to pay much attention to 'the worst of all subjects, ones self' (c, 196).

Part vi of *The Theory of Moral Sentiments* outlines three types of virtue, beginning with the virtue of prudence. Smith defines prudence as 'care of the health, of the fortune, of the rank and reputation of the individual, the objects upon which his comfort and happiness in this life are supposed principally to depend' (*TMS*, 213). The prudent man puts his security first, and hence goes about bettering his condition, not through risky speculations but by first cultivating 'real knowledge and skill' in his chosen profession and then practising it with 'assiduity and industry'. He also displays a 'frugality' that meets the full approval of the Impartial Spectator because it involves deferring the modicum of 'ease and enjoyment' he could enjoy now for 'a more distant but more lasting' ease to be had later. The prudent man's conversation may not be sprightly, but he is polite without being showy, honest without being candid, more 'capable of friendship' than sociable (*TMS*, 214–15).

The prudent man's attention to his own affairs brings him a real tranquillity, which he prefers to the 'vain splendour' that ambition offers to the Poor Man's Son. While the Poor Man's Son sacrifices his present and future tranquillity in return for the instruments of happiness (not actual happiness), the prudent man enriches himself without sacrificing tranquillity. Though he is a good man of business, you will not find him obsessed with profit – that is, 'laying a plot either to gain or to save a single shilling'. Such an obsession with pecuniary gain 'would degrade the most vulgar tradesman in the opinion of all his neighbours' (*TMS*, 173). He is never insolent, never puts himself before other people. Unfortunately his preference for tranquillity also leads him to neglect 'the real and solid glory of performing the greatest and most magnanimous actions'. This limitation is the reason why this prudence is never considered 'one of the most endearing, or of the most ennobling of the virtues. It commands a certain cold esteem, but seems not entitled to any very ardent love or admiration' (*TMS*, 216).

Only when we move beyond the prudent man does Smith begin to speak of 'the wise and virtuous man'. The phrase is striking. One

The first plate of William Hogarth's *Industry and Idleness*, 1747. Sober habits will make the Industrious Apprentice (centre) a prudent employer and Lord Mayor.

might have thought virtue enough in and of itself. Smith follows Aristotle in seeing virtue as a question of action rather than a state of being. He disdains those 'whining and melancholy moralists' who claim to feel for all humans, regardless of whether they are capable of offering those humans any assistance. Beneficence (doing good) was far preferable to benevolence (well-wishing). Perhaps Smith's emphasis on the role of judgement and his view of virtue as linked to an ability or faculty of making judgements (judgements of propriety, first and foremost) leads him to couple virtue with wisdom. Perhaps the yoking together of virtue and wisdom also reflects Smith's recognition of the need to allow for human fallibility, unintended consequences and chance, all of which might render it inadvisable to follow the promptings of virtue all of the time. Smith can thus write of how it requires 'the highest effort of political wisdom' for a wise patriot to determine whether it is better in times of 'public discontent' to 're-establish the authority of the old system' or attempt to establish a new constitutional regime (*TMS*, 231–2). This wisdom is not obscurely theoretical, but practical and above all 'politic', in the now rare sense of that adjective: 'judicious, expedient, sensible'.[2]

The two other virtues are addressed, not to the individual's own happiness but that of others. The first of these is self-command, or magnanimity (literally 'greatness of soul'). The *Oxford English Dictionary* defines magnanimity as a 'well-founded high regard for oneself manifesting as generosity of spirit and equanimity in the face of trouble', as well as 'greatness of thought or purpose; grandeur or nobility of designs, ambition, spirit'.[3] Jacques-Louis David's famous painting in the Louvre *The Lictors Bring to Brutus the Bodies of his Sons* (1787) depicts an example of magnanimity. Showing heroic self-command and putting the security of the Roman Republic before his own family, the statesmanlike Brutus orders the death of his sons when they attempt a coup. In contrast to the retiring prudent man, the magnanimous man actively seeks

Jacques-Louis David, study for *The Lictors Bring to Brutus the Bodies of His Sons*, 1787, black chalk, pen and ink. Brutus (front left) magnanimously puts the good of the Republic before his affection for his sons.

the praise of others, and hence craves their attention, too. This leads him to seek glory, which receives a warm rather than cold esteem:

> The desire for the esteem and admiration of other people,
> when for qualities and talents which are the natural
> and proper objects of esteem and admiration, is the real
> love of true glory; a passion which, if not the very best
> passion of human nature, is certainly one of the best.

To win this esteem the individual must restrain those passions that flare up at rare moments of great tension (fear and anger) as well as those that constantly seek to seduce us (the love of pleasure and praise). This self-command is most obvious in times of ferment; epic struggles and conflicts among great empires and nations have their echo in 'warfare within the breast', of a kind that may be too much for sensitive or emotional people. It demands a certain 'hardiness and firmness of temper' (TMS, 245).

The prudent man has no need of 'fortune' when he can achieve his modest goal with 'no loss or hazard' (TMS, 213). Smith insists that hard work and other prudent habits will always pay off in the long run. As for the (very) short run, the basic decencies are easily acquired, and the true pleasures of tranquillity are almost always at hand. 'Hazard' or 'fortune' enter only when 'ambition' rears its head, tormenting us with visions – of great wealth, which cannot be reached by hard work alone, and of adulation, which the prudent man's modest circle of family and true friends cannot offer. Luck has 'great influence over the moral sentiments of mankind', Smith notes. Whether we perceive a certain character with 'love and admiration' or 'universal hatred and contempt' is often just a question of whether they succeeded or failed in their endeavours. Magnanimity also carries with it the risk of 'excessive self-admiration', which success can take to ludicrous heights. Like Smith's example of Alexander the Great, these individuals can come to see themselves as gods, displaying a foolish vanity and insolence towards other humans (TMS, 250).

Prudence and magnanimity both depend on the sentiments of others, in so far as our estimation of our own merit is derived from others' sympathy and praise. The virtue of beneficence leads us to consider 'the idea of exact propriety and perfection, so far as we are each of us capable of comprehending that idea'. This idea is incorporated as the Impartial Spectator, 'the great demigod within the breast, the great judge and arbiter of conduct'. The portrait or likeness of this Impartial Spectator 'is in every man more or less accurately drawn, its colouring . . . more or less just, its outlines . . . more or less exactly designed' (TMS, 247). The 'wise and virtuous' man is the man able to spend more time on these refinements. Rather than taking increasing pride in its appearance, he becomes more aware of his failings to equal it in his actual behaviour. This is because the process renders him more sensitive to gradations of imperfection that those inferior to him cannot perceive. As Smith notes:

> In all the liberal and ingenious arts, in painting, in poetry, in music, in eloquence, in philosophy, the great artist feels always the real imperfection of his own best works, and is more sensible than any man how much they fall short of that ideal perfection of which he has formed some conception, which he imitates as well as he can, but which he despairs of ever equalling. It is the inferior artist only, who is ever perfectly satisfied with his own performances (*TMS*, 248).

Readers who are visual artists can judge the accuracy of this statement for themselves.

The rest of us are probably more able to relate it to an activity Smith might not have considered an art, but which nonetheless represents the only activity in which most readers are likely to experience the demands of artistry: cookery. That the best cooks are the first and best critics of their own work is an observation almost trite. It is clear to their fortunate if puzzled guests that the host's anxious questions about whether the meal would not taste the better for some adjustment are rhetorical. They are not motivated by a love of praise or a bid for sympathetic sorrow, but are based on contemplation of fine nuances that their audience probably cannot taste. To attempt to comfort such a cook by saying, 'Don't worry, this is so much better than anything I could cook' is to miss the point. The cook is not competing with their guests or even trying to produce an 'above-average meal', but rather endeavouring to reach perfection. While compliments are a social custom (useful in instilling gratitude), praise and even sympathetic grief (at failing, yet again, to achieve perfection) are neither wanted nor desired. There is a forgetfulness of self – at least, of that self composed with regard to others. The self is transcended. Most of us know someone capable of achieving this transcendence at a dinner party. Smith is hardly asking for the moon.

This 'wise and virtuous man' does not look down on those less virtuous than he, nor does he pander to the rich and powerful. 'He is never so elated as to look down with insolence even upon those who are really below him. He feels so well his own imperfection, he knows so well the difficulty with which he attained his own distant approximation to rectitude, that he cannot regard with contempt the still greater imperfection of other people' (*TMS*, 248). This beneficence thus lacks that tendency towards 'insolence' and vanity Smith notes among those who put themselves forward for risky enterprises, in which they ostentatiously sacrifice their own interests for those of others.

It also lacks that sullen pride that Smith identifies in the Stoics, which Plato noted in Diogenes when the latter trampled on his fine carpets: prickly, unsociable, disdaining the respect shown to 'rank and fortune', 'convinced of his own superiority' yet unwilling 'to explain the grounds of his own pretensions' (*TMS*, 255). However sublime the resulting thoughts, as far as Smith is concerned a Diogenes-style retreat from society is no excuse for 'the neglect of the smallest active duty' (*TMS*, 237). On a personal level, Smith sought to find a middle way between the tendency to vanity he noted in his friend Hume, and the tendency to pride obvious in Rousseau – tendencies Smith's fellow Scot Allan Ramsay captured in his respective portraits of them.

As we have seen, it can seem as if Smith's morality puts any sense of 'inner' or 'true' emotional life beyond investigation. We are a series of performances, which become more persuasive the more adept we become at approximating a range of other individuals' emotional states. This was the basis of Rousseau's complaint against commercial society: that it created a society based on dissimulation (that is, acting), one where 'there is but mummery in even honour, friendship, virtue, and often vice itself', where humans are 'always asking others what we are, and never daring to ask ourselves'.[4] Yet Smith's wise and virtuous man can, it seems, step out of this hall of mirrors and find a place to *be*, without retreating to a barrel like Diogenes. As the historian Ryan Patrick Hanley has observed, the virtues of prudence, magnanimity and benevolence can be understood as offering an interlocking 'dialectical account of ethical virtue', each compensating for the excesses or limitations of the others.[5] The three might be seen as leading us 'upwards', out of ourselves and closer to godlike benevolence. But it might be more helpful to see them as a circle, leading us back to prudence – not the prudence that earned but a 'cold esteem' but what Smith calls 'superior prudence'.

It is here that Smith explains his preference for the couplet of 'wisdom and virtue':

> Wise and judicious conduct, when directed to greater and nobler purposes than the care of the health, the fortune, the rank and reputation of the individual, is frequently and very properly called prudence. We talk of the prudence of the great general, of the great statesman, of the great legislator. Prudence is, in all these cases, combined with many greater and more splendid virtues, with valour, with extensive and strong benevolence, with a sacred regard to the rules of justice, and all these supported by a proper degree of self-command. This superior prudence, when carried to the highest degree of perfection, necessarily supposes the art, the talent, and the habit or disposition of acting with the most perfect propriety in every possible circumstance and situation. It necessarily supposes the utmost perfection of all the intellectual and all of the moral virtues. It is the best head joined to the best heart. It is the most perfect wisdom combined with the most perfect virtue (*TMS*, 216).

The 'wise and virtuous man' has become one with the Impartial Spectator.

In the two centuries following Smith's death his approach to virtue and justice was not widely followed, something that must have played a role in the separation of *The Wealth of Nations* and *The Theory of Moral Sentiments* by leading political economists. One camp of ethicists followed Hume's utility-focused line, often described as 'consequentialist' in that it evaluates actions according to their capacity to maximize 'the greatest happiness of the greatest number' (as the utilitarian Jeremy Bentham put it). As we have seen, Smith saw utility as a rationalization that revealed more about our taste for systems than our motivations. Another camp placed virtue in universal, reason-based moral rules – the 'deontological' line, based on Immanuel Kant. Smith recognized that, far from being universal, moral rules varied from one stage of human development to another, influenced by custom and even fashion. To that extent his approach is descriptive rather than normative. Yet Smith also differs from Kant in the authority he gives to 'Nature'. This is not the nature of 'natural rights', but that which implants certain instincts and dispositions: to share passions, to 'truck, barter and exchange', to seek to persuade others and so on. Whether these instincts and dispositions are the same as those that reason or utility might suggest is neither here nor there to Smith. To this extent Smith is normative, although the influence of custom and fashion makes it hard for us to say exactly where normative nature and descriptive history (or, perhaps better, sociology) begins.

One example of the 'irregularity of Nature' takes us back to our consideration of sympathy and the Impartial Spectator. Imagine that you accidentally bump into someone. Our first reaction is immediately to say 'sorry!' Indeed, in Britain one might well find that the other person also says 'sorry!' (Americans have certainly noticed this habit, and find it amusing). For us (the bumper) to apologize to the bumped makes no sense, Smith points out, because we obviously did not intend to bump into them and no reasonable person could attribute such an intention to us (Smith assumes that the bumper is not rushing through a crowd heedlessly, which would, of course, suggest a disrespect for others walking on the same street). The fact that the bumper apologizes demonstrates that 'even the impartial spectator' goes along with 'what may be regarded as the unjust resentment of that other', that is, the resentment of the bumped (*TMS*, 104). Here Nature is leading us to act in an unreasonable and unjust manner.

This apparent 'irregularity of Nature' reflects the fact that 'the world judges by the event, and not by the design.' Kant would later insist that it was only the 'design' (or intention) that determined whether an action was deemed right or wrong. Smith recognizes that the failure of the 'world' to put design first has 'been in all ages the complaint, and is the great discouragement of virtue' (*TMS*, 105). Strong words. But Smith insists that this apparent irregularity is resolved: 'Nature, however, when she implanted the seeds of this irregularity in the human breast, seems, as upon all other occasions, to have intended the happiness and perfection of the species . . . [if] sentiments, thoughts, intentions, would become the objects of punishment . . . every court of judicature would become a real inquisition' (*TMS*, 105). Our very thoughts could land us in court. Indeed, this 'irregularity' served utility by leading us to prefer beneficence over benevolence, reminds us that humans were 'made for action'.

The 'irregularity' also taught man to 'reverence the happiness of his brethren'. It is on this 'irregularity' that Smith grounds what we might call human dignity, that special status that all human beings enjoy simply on account of being alive. This is something that philosophers might otherwise struggle with. That 'dread' humans feel of harming others and so being the object of their resentment, which explains our irrational apology for bumping into someone, has wide ramifications:

As, in the ancient heathen religion, that holy ground which had been consecrated to some god, was not to be trod upon but upon solemn and necessary occasions, and the man who had even ignorantly violated it, became piacular [sinful, blamable] from that moment, and, until proper atonement should be made, incurred the vengeance of that powerful and invisible being to whom it had been set apart; so, by the wisdom of Nature, the happiness of every innocent man is, in the same manner, rendered holy, consecrated, and hedged round against the approach of every other man; not to be wantonly trod upon, not even to be, in any respect, ignorantly and involuntarily violated, without requiring some expiation, some atonement in proportion to the greatness of such undesigned violation (TMS, 107).

Though not in Part vi of *The Theory of Moral Sentiments*, this passage was one of the important additions Smith made to the sixth edition. Smith had already used earlier editions to depict this remorse in lurid colours, describing it as 'of all the sentiments which can enter the human breast the most dreadful'. The power of this passion, he wrote, reflected the importance of justice as 'the main pillar' upholding society. Compared to it, beneficence is but 'ornamentation' (TMS, 85–6).

Is this view of human dignity related to a Christian injunction to 'love your neighbour as yourself'? As we have seen, Smith's view of self is so 'un-selfish' that he seems to put things the other way around: 'As to love our neighbour as we love ourselves is the great law of Christianity,' Smith notes, 'so it is the great precept of nature to love ourselves only as we love our neighbour, or what comes to the same thing, as our neighbour is capable of loving us' (TMS, 25). Whereas Christianity assumes that we originally have self-love, and must be told to direct a similar passion towards those around us, nature makes us so beholden to others for the composition of our self that such prior self-love is impossible. This is not the only area where Smith implicitly challenges a Christian view, while at the same time veiling this in Christian language. He can thus write of the 'all-wise Author of Nature' (God) leading us to desire our fellow humans' praise more than His own. God 'has made man, if I may say so, the immediate judge of mankind; and has, in this respect, as in many others, created him after his own image, and appointed him his viceregent on earth, to superintend the behaviour of his brethren' (*TMS*, 130).

Smith is traditional enough to ascribe male gender to God and to describe man as created 'in the image of God', but defers divine judgement, or rather makes it a function of our sense of resentment in response to injustice. The fact that all religions have their heavens and hells, Smith writes, demonstrates how this 'sense' pursues injustice 'if I may say so, even beyond the grave, though the example of its punishment there cannot serve to deter the rest of mankind, who see it not, who know it not, from being guilty of the like practices here'. Smith is not only claiming, *pace* Pufendorf and most of his contemporaries, that belief in the afterlife does not lead to virtuous behaviour on earth; he is explaining the concept as in effect a superstition that 'Nature' and 'religion' (viewed anthropologically) impose on us (*TMS*, 91).

Two hundred years after Smith's death his thought began to seem 'relevant' to philosophers, as well as to those who might be called neuroeconomists. To some extent these trends have been opposed to each other. Smith's interest in the philosophy of mind and in the apparent irrational or non-utilitarian manner in which we feel resentment (and so 'punish' and 'reward' others) appeals to economists interested in engaging with neuroscientists such as those exploring the function of mirror neurons. Here Smith's appeal to 'nature' and the 'species' are far from being liabilities, while his interest in the development of human society appeals to those eager to understand human behaviour as the product of human evolution. These developments are not welcomed by philosophers, many of whom fear that bandying about images from fMRI scans and talk about 'memes' represent so many excesses of a form of scientism that Raymond Tallis has dubbed 'neuromania' and 'Darwinitis'.[6] Human consciousness and human culture (what Matthew Arnold called 'the best which has been thought and said') cannot be explained in such terms, philosophers contend, nor should they be allowed to restrict our limitless potential.

The newfound interest in Smith exhibited among philosophers is related to the revival of a third approach to ethics, known as virtue ethics: one that addresses moral character and behaviour rather than utility or reason. Smith's focus on human faculties of judging (according to a standard of propriety, merit and so on) rather than on moral absolutes clearly places him in this tradition, as does his admiration of Aristotle, held to be the founder of this approach. The contemporary revival of virtue ethics originated in Alasdair MacIntyre's *After Virtue* (1981) and continues in the work of the Nobel Prize-winning economist and philosopher Amartya Sen.

Sen's *The Idea of Justice* (2009) saw him propose an approach to justice founded on Smith's Impartial Spectator. He contrasted this with the highly influential model created by John Rawls, who bases just action on judgements of 'fairness' made from an 'original position' located behind a 'veil of ignorance'. According to this hypothetical scenario, Rawls imagines a group of people meeting to determine the socio-economic structure of society, in entire ignorance of their own age, gender, skills, intelligence, religion, race and wealth. What kind of society would they establish, or what decision would they reach about a specific issue if they found themselves in this position? Although Rawls had himself cited Smith in his landmark *A Theory of Justice* (1971), Sen noted the important differences between the operation of Rawls's 'veil' and Smith's Impartial Spectator, arguing that the latter offered a more helpful basis for reaching decisions about how to create a fair world order. Sen identified Rawls with a tradition of 'transcendental institutionalism' dating back to Hobbes, Locke, Rousseau and Kant, one focused on identifying what perfect justice would look like and intent on 'getting the institutions right' rather than considering 'the actual societies that would ultimately emerge'.

Smith, Sen claims, followed an approach of 'realization-focused comparison', attentive to 'actual institutions, actual behaviour and other influences', and drawn to contrasting multiple existing or feasible societies.[7] Drawing on Smith, Sen makes a number of assertions about how best to serve 'the cause of justice': that it is not necessary to have a concept of perfect justice to determine if this or that measure would enhance justice; that concepts of fairness exist prior to any principles of justice humans might develop; that Smithian 'open' impartiality (the Impartial Spectator does not necessarily belong to the deliberating group) is better in addressing global challenges than Rawlsian 'closed' impartiality.[8]

This is not the place to referee between Sen and Rawls. What is nonetheless clear is that the failure of Smith to use the terminology of social contract and his reluctance to delineate an ideal set of institutions are now being seen as strengths rather than weaknesses.[9] Rawls's veil of ignorance may be intellectually sophisticated, but it is also very alien to our lived experience as humans. How can we imagine ourselves as deliberating, disembodied humans and at the same time situate ourselves relative to equally virtual members of a yet-to-be-established ideal community? Smith's Impartial Spectator admittedly represents a somewhat forbidding ideal. But Smith shows us how we can reach it, led partly by our innate motivations and partly by a process of virtuous self-cultivation. There are no dramatic leaps of the imagination, unlike the fantastic leap Rawls demands of us.

And what of that disembodied member, the famous 'invisible hand'? It may be helpful to follow Emma Rothschild in seeing it as 'ironic . . . in its intimation of the existence of an all-ordering providence', but 'unironic, in its intimation that there can be order without design; that a society can be prosperous without being conducted by an all-seeing sovereign.' Like Smith's beautiful utilitarian systems, it is a powerful persuasive device and, as Rothschild puts it, 'a sort of trinket'.[10] As she notes, the risk of adopting 'invisible hand explanations' is the risk of missing this joke – and reproducing the very attitude of disdain for the individual motivations of the pieces on the great board of human society Smith intended to satirize. If free-market economics has led the world to prosper while releasing individuals from crushing dependence, then that is to be credited to 'the universal progress of opulence' that Smith explains in terms of a web of interlocking instincts and desires that the 'invisible hand' does not fully capture.

The progress of opulence is not limitless, however. There will come a point at which a nation reaches its 'full complement of riches'. This point is not the same for all nations, Smith says. The degree to which a nation can absorb capital and put it to work, is related to its 'laws and institutions'. An economic question cannot be divorced from consideration of the society more broadly, even its fashions. To demonstrate this, Smith contrasts what were then two very different countries: Holland, a restless republic in constant danger of being swallowed up by the sea but whose many ships criss-crossed the globe; and China, a vast agricultural empire widely held to be tranquil and happy (French *philosophes* admired Confucius greatly).

In contrast to Holland, China was 'a country which neglects or despises foreign commerce'. It was also one in which 'the poor or the owners of small capitals' enjoyed much less security than 'the rich or the owners of large capitals', being subjected to being 'pillaged and plundered' by mandarins 'under the pretence of justice' (*WN*, 112–13). Thanks to this 'oppression' the rich could monopolize what trade there was, and enjoy a whacking 12 per cent interest on their capital. This high rate led Smith to conclude that China had reached 'that full complement of riches which is consistent with the nature of its laws and institutions' (*WN*, 111). Today it is the Communist Party mandarins that 'pillage and plunder' the poor of China, expropriating common land, evicting those living on it and developing it for thir own interests, without the least 'pretence of justice'.

For Smith, Holland illustrates the advantages of a society whose 'laws and institutions' allowed it to absorb a large quantity of capital. Here the interest rate is much lower than in China (at 3 per cent); so low, indeed, that nobody can just lend out their capital and support themselves on the interest they receive.

> In a country which had acquired its full complement of riches, where in every particular branch of business there was the greatest quantity of stock that could be employed in it, as the ordinary rate of clear profit would be very small, so the usual market rate of interest which could be afforded out of it, would be so low as to render it impossible for any but the very wealthiest people to live upon the interest of their money. All people of small or middling fortunes would be obliged to superintend themselves the employment of their own stocks. It would be necessary that almost every man should be a man of business, or engage in some sort of trade. The province of Holland seems to be approaching near to this state. It is there unfashionable not to be a man of business. Necessity makes it usual for almost every man to be so, and custom every where regulates fashion. As it is ridiculous not to dress, so is it, in some measure, not to be employed, like other people. As a man of a civil profession seems aukward in a camp or a garrison, and is even in some danger of being despised there, so does an idle man among men of business (*WN*, 113).

Even those without capital were better off, as the wages in Holland were, Smith remarked, higher than in England. Admittedly, few

Dutch merchants were willing to confirm that trade was booming. As always, men of business whined to any statesman willing to listen about how hard things were for the economy: 'When profit diminishes, merchants are very apt to complain that trade decays; though the diminution of profit is the natural effect of its prosperity.' All the 'symptoms' pointed to one conclusion: 'there is no general decay' (*wn*, 108). Whereas Marx would claim that capitalism resulted in a society divided between a small rentier class of employers and a mass of labourers, Smith claims that where the 'laws and institutions' permit, nobody will be allowed to be idle. Nobody will even want to *appear* idle.

Quite why competition among capital has yet to lead to such a state is a question Smith might struggle to answer to our complete satisfaction. He would be frustrated by the prevalence of joint-stock companies over 'private copartneries' (private partnerships). The 'total exemption from trouble and from risk, beyond a limited sum', Smith notes in *The Wealth of Nations*, 'encourages many people to become adventurers in joint stock companies', people of a sort who would never venture to start their own private business (*wn*, 741). Apart from the sectors of banking, insurance, infrastructure and utilities, which legitimately demand large amounts of capital and which 'are capable of being reduced to what [is] called a Routine', Smith is opposed to joint-stock companies (*wn*, 756). The travails of notorious eighteenth-century British joint-stock companies such as the South Sea Company and the East India Company did not instil much confidence. Yet today the world economy is dominated by such firms, largely thanks to the Victorian invention of limited liability, which reduced the risks to individual investors.

Smith might also point to the many ways in which 'freedom of trade' is very far indeed from being realized in today's world, for all the heat generated about globalization. His own hopes of seeing it established even in his home nation were not great. 'To expect, indeed, that the freedom of trade should ever be entirely restored in Great Britain,' he notes in *The Wealth of Nations*, 'is as absurd as to expect that an Oceana or Utopia should ever be established in it' (*WN*, 471). Mercantilist lobbying of government has become a trade in itself, fine-tuning the vast 'bounties' enjoyed by agriculture and other privileged sectors both in the European Union and particularly in the United States, where it has corrupted the entire political system. Elsewhere, from Brazil through Russia to China, a hybrid form of state capitalism has created a new class of mandarins who domineer over those outside their tightly knit web of party- or court-focused patronage, depriving them of the security necessary for them to be able to enrich themselves through more prudent enterprise.

In his landmark book *Capital in the Twenty-first Century*, first published in French in 2013, the economist Thomas Piketty conceded that competition among capital would lower levels of return – but only in the very long term, when there was nowhere left to invest one's capital. Piketty's analysis is based on the observation that over centuries 'the rate of return on capital was always at least 10 to 20 times greater than the rate of growth of output (and income)'.[11] Instead of ushering in a new age of capitalism in which inflation and the rise of 'human capital' would destroy the rentier class, the ruptures of two world wars and post-war inflation had masked this and other underlying constants, which indicate a return to early nineteenth-century norms familiar from the novels of Jane Austen, where inheritance and marriage overshadow individual skill and entrepreneurialism as factors determining an individual's wealth. In this early nineteenth-century world the top 10 per cent owned 80 per cent of total wealth, and the top 1 per cent owned 55 per cent.

With his characteristic acuity, Gordon Gekko had noticed the way things were going in 1987:

The richest one percent of this country owns half our country's wealth, five trillion dollars. One third of that

comes from hard work, two thirds comes from inheritance,
interest on interest accumulating to widows and idiot
sons and what I do, stock and real estate speculation. It's
bullshit. You got ninety percent of the American public out
there with little or no net worth. I create nothing. I own.

Piketty's figures, if anything, make Gekko's estimate of the
concentration of capital look conservative. In the decades since
1977 the growth of the U.S. economy had floated all boats, but some
boats floated much higher than others. The richest 1 per cent took
60 per cent of the growth in national income, amassing fabulous
fortunes; the bottom 90 per cent saw growth, too, but at a rate of
income growth less than 0.5 per cent a year.[12] Rather than building
up savings in middle life in order to spend them in retirement,
dying with next to nothing (the 'Modigliani triangle' model), these
rentiers can live very well on a sliver of their capital income, and
reinvest the rest for their heirs.

Thanks to tax havens and excellent investment advice, owners
of large capitals pay much less in tax and enjoy much higher returns
on investment income than the rest. The larger the capital, the
higher the return on the capital. Piketty makes this point with
reference to American universities (unlike the super-wealthy, such
institutions have to publish figures about their endowments):
over the past thirty years the three largest university endowments
have earned a fantastic average annual rate of return of 10.2 per
cent per year – while the 498 universities with endowments of
less than $100 million received just 6.2 per cent.[13] The author's
bank is currently offering an 'attractive' rate of 1.3 per cent.

Piketty is concerned that, left unchecked, such inequalities in
income might reach a point at which either society breaks down or
governments use capital controls and other means to reintroduce
protectionism. 'Inequality is not necessarily bad in itself', he notes,
'the key question is to decide whether it is justified, whether there

are reasons for it.'[14] While Piketty proposes some practical steps we might take to address these problems, an exclusive focus on money and ownership inevitably leaves out many of the other, less quantifiable factors that arguably have as much of an impact on where and how we perceive inequality, how we feel about it and how those feelings might lead us to act or vote in certain ways. For 'economics' as a discipline, however, Piketty is yet another sign that the intellectual tide is running Smith's way. Indeed, Piketty prefers the 'old-fashioned' label 'political economy', which, he says, 'conveys the only thing that sets economics apart from the other social sciences: its political, normative, and moral purpose'.[15] He provides ample food for an interdisciplinary discussion, not only with fellow social scientists but with philosophers and neuroscientists. Smith's works suggest a number of directions such a discussion might take – and reminds us to be sceptical of anyone offering cast-iron certainties.

After all, the 'progress of opulence' and the development of human society are processes that we can never fully perceive or understand, let alone control. Rather than a source of anxiety, Smith sees this as evidence of the underlying resilience of mankind. Human society has taken many different forms at many different times and in many different places, without falling apart into chaos.

It is thus that man, who can subsist only in society, was fitted by nature to that situation for which he was made. All the members of human society stand in need of each others assistance, and are likewise exposed to mutual injuries. Where the necessary assistance is reciprocally afforded from love, from gratitude, from friendship, and esteem, the society flourishes and is happy. All the different members of it are bound together by the agreeable bands of love and affection, and are, as it were, drawn to one common centre of mutual good offices. But though the necessary assistance should not be afforded from such generous and disinterested motives, though among the different members of the society there should be no mutual love and affection, the society, though less happy and agreeable, will not necessarily be dissolved. Society may subsist among different men, as among different merchants, from a sense of its utility, without any mutual love or affection; and though no man in it should owe any obligation, or be bound in gratitude to any other, it may still be upheld by a mercenary exchange of good offices according to an agreed valuation (*TMS*, 85–6).

After Smith's death it was assumed that his thought sought to encourage this 'mercenary exchange'. Thanks to the revival of interest in *The Theory of Moral Sentiments* as well as recent work in neuroscience, economics and philosophy, we recognize that in fact Smith considered this rational world to be second-best. With Smith's head, heart and hand, we can reorient ourselves towards this 'one common centre'.

References

Introduction

1 Donald Winch, 'Darwin Fallen among the Political Economists', *Proceedings of the American Philosophical Society*, CXLV (2001), pp. 415–37.
2 Immanuel Kant, 'An Answer to the Question: What is Enlightenment?', *Practical Philosophy*, ed. and trans. Mary J. Gregor (Cambridge, 1996), pp. 11–22; available at www.marxists.org (accessed 27 May 2015).
3 Charles L. Griswold Jr, *Adam Smith and the Virtues of Enlightenment* (Cambridge, 1999), p. 2.
4 For the 1356 and 1497 ordinances quoted here, see Barbara Megson, *The Pinners' and Wiresellers' Book, 1462–1511* (London, 2009).
5 Diogenes Laertius, *Lives of Eminent Philosophers*, ed. and trans. R. D. Hicks, vol. II (London, 1925), p. 26.
6 Dugald Stewart, *Biographical Memoirs of Adam Smith* (Edinburgh, 1877).
7 Cited in D. D. Raphael and A. L. Macfie, 'Introduction', *TMS*, p. 28.

1 The Theatre of Nature, 1723–50

1 Alex J. Warden, *The Linen Trade* (London, 1864), p. 480.
2 E. G. West, *Adam Smith: The Man and his Works* (Indianapolis, IN, 1976), p. 35.
3 Samuel von Pufendorf, *The Whole Duty of Man According to the Law of Nature*, ed. Ian Hunter and David Saunders, trans. Andrew Tooke (Indianapolis, IN, 2003), Book 1, chapter 4, section 9.
4 Francis Hutcheson, *On Human Nature*, ed. Thomas Mautner (Cambridge, 1993), p. 131.

5 Francis Hutcheson, *An Essay on the Nature and Conduct of the Passions and Affections, with Illustrations on the Moral Sense*, ed. Aaron Garrett (Indianapolis, IN, 2002), p. 17.

6 Hutcheson, *On Human Nature*, p. 105.

7 Ibid., p. 136.

8 Denis Diderot, 'Éloge de Richardson', original published in *Journal étranger* [January 1762], from *Selected Writings on Art and Literature*, trans. Geoffrey Bremner (London, 1994).

9 David Hume, *A Treatise of Human Nature*, ed. David Fate Norton and Mary J. Norton (Oxford, 2000), p. 261.

10 Hume to Hutcheson, 17 September 1739, in J.Y.T. Greig, *The Letters of David Hume*, vol. I (Oxford, 1932), p. 32.

11 Ibid., p. 206.

12 Ibid., p. 266.

13 Ibid., p. 203.

14 Ibid., pp. 321, 370.

15 Cited in Nicholas Phillipson, *Adam Smith: An Enlightened Life* (London, 2011), p. 104.

16 Cited ibid., p. 85.

2 Spectatorship and Sympathy, 1751–63

1 Ian Campbell Ross, *The Life of Adam Smith* (Oxford, 1995), p. 118.

2 Ibid., p. 194.

3 Ralph S. Walker, ed., *Correspondence of James Boswell and John Johnston of Grange* (New York, 1966), p. 7.

4 John Rae, *Life of Adam Smith* (London, 1895), p. 36.

5 Cited in Nicholas Phillipson, *Adam Smith: An Enlightened Life* (London, 2011), pp. 132–3.

6 Mbemba Jabbi, Marte Swart and Christian Keysers, 'Empathy for Positive and Negative Emotions in the Gustatory Cortex', *NeuroImage*, XXXIV/4 (2007), pp. 1744–53.

7 David Hume, *A Treatise of Human Nature*, ed. David Fate Norton and Mary J. Norton (Oxford, 2000), p. 309.

8 'compose, *v.*' (definition III, 17a), *OED*, www.oed.com, accessed 19 January 2015.

9   Ullrich Wagner et al., 'Beautiful Friendship: Social Sharing of
     Emotions Improves Subjective Feelings and Activates the Neural
     Reward Circuitry', *Social Cognitive and Affective Neuroscience* (2014):
     nsu121v2-nsu121.
10 'compose, *v.*' (definition 1, 3 and 4), OED, www.oed.com, accessed
     19 January 2015.
11 Hume, *Treatise of Human Nature*, p. 384.

3 Trading Places, 1764–6

1   Ian Campbell Ross, 'Educating an Eighteenth-century Duke', in *The
     Scottish Tradition: Essays in Honour of R. G. Cant*, ed. G.W.S. Barrow
     (Edinburgh, 1974), p. 185.
2   Nicholas Phillipson, *Adam Smith: An Enlightened Life* (London, 2011),
     p. 183.
3   Ian Campbell Ross, *The Life of Adam Smith* (Oxford, 1995), p. 200.
4   See Steven L. Kaplan, *Bread, Politics and Political Economy in the Reign
     of Louis XV* (The Hague, 1976).
5   Jean-Jacques Rousseau, *The Social Contract and Discourses,* trans.
     G.D.H. Cole (London, 1973), p. 70.
6   Ibid., p. 84.
7   Ibid., p. 92.

4 Golden Dreams, 1767–75

1   Cited in Brian Bonnyman, *The Third Duke of Buccleuch and Adam
     Smith: Estate Management and Improvement in Enlightenment Scotland*
     (Edinburgh, 2014), p. 126.
2   See Henry Hamilton, 'The Failure of the Ayr Bank, 1772', *Economic
     History Review*, n. s., III (1956), pp. 405–17.
3   Bonnyman, *The Third Duke of Buccleuch*, pp. 80–81.
4   Ian Campbell Ross, *The Life of Adam Smith* (Oxford, 1995), p. 284.

5 The Machine of Government, 1776–89

1 Knud Haakonssen, *The Science of a Legislator: The Natural Jurisprudence of David Hume and Adam Smith* (Cambridge, 1981), p. 118.
2 Karl Marx, *Economic and Philosophic Manuscripts of 1844*, trans. Martin Mulligan (Moscow, 1959), p. 63.

Conclusion: Head, Heart and Hand, 1790

1 Jean M. Twenge and W. Kevin Campbell, *The Narcissism Epidemic: Living in the Age of Entitlement* (New York, 2009), p. 13. See also Jean M. Twenge and Tim Kasser, 'Generational Changes in Materialism and Work Centrality, 1976–2007: Associations with Temporal Changes in Societal Insecurity and Materialistic Role Modeling', *Personality and Social Psychology Bulletin*, xxxix/7 (July 2013), pp. 883–97.
2 'politic, *adj*. and *n*.' (definition 2.a), *OED*, www.oed.com, accessed 28 January 2015.
3 'magnanimity, *n*.', ibid.
4 Jean-Jacques Rousseau, *The Social Contract and Discourses*, trans. G.D.H. Cole (London, 1973), p. 116.
5 Ryan Patrick Hanley, *Adam Smith and the Character of Virtue* (Cambridge, 2009), p. 163.
6 Raymond Tallis, *Aping Mankind: Neuromania, Darwinitis and the Misrepresentation of Humanity* (London, 2011).
7 Amartya Sen, *The Idea of Justice* (London, 2009), pp. 6–7.
8 Ibid., pp. ix, 81, 123.
9 For a different view, however, see D. D. Raphael, *The Impartial Spectator: Adam Smith's Moral Philosophy* (Oxford, 2007), pp. 31, 48.
10 Emma Rothschild, *Economic Sentiments: Adam Smith, Condorcet, and the Enlightenment* (Cambridge, MA, 2001), pp. 135 (ironic), 137 (trinket).
11 Thomas Piketty, *Capital in the Twenty-first Century*, trans. Arthur Goldhammer (Cambridge, MA, 2014), pp. 353 (quotation), 366.
12 Ibid., pp. 344 (fig. 10.3), 297.
13 Ibid., p. 448 (table 12.2).
14 Ibid., p. 19.
15 Ibid., p. 574.

Further Reading

All the volumes in the Glasgow Edition of the Works and Correspondence of Adam Smith are available in inexpensive paperback form from Liberty Fund Press, with their original notes, apparatus and excellent introductory essays. Henry C. Clark's edited volume *Commerce, Culture and Liberty: Readings on Capitalism before Adam Smith* (Indianapolis, IN, 2003) offers a useful reader of seventeenth- and eighteenth-century French, Dutch and English texts on mercantilism, luxury, trade and related topics. Inexpensive yet scholarly editions of the works of Hutcheson, Hume and even Kames are also available from the Liberty Fund.

Although E. G. West's *Adam Smith: The Man and His Works* (Indianapolis, IN, 1976) and Ian Simpson Ross's *The Life of Adam Smith* (Oxford, 1995) may still be read with pleasure and profit, the definitive biography of Smith is now Nicholas Phillipson's *Adam Smith: An Enlightened Life* (London, 2010). Those interested in Smith's relationship with the Duke of Buccleuch and Scottish agricultural improvement will find Brian Bonnyman's *The Third Duke of Buccleuch and Adam Smith* (Edinburgh, 2014) of interest, while those of us with the imagination and whimsy to speculate on what Smith might make of our own times will enjoy *Saving Adam Smith: A Tale of Wealth, Transformation and Virtue* by Jonathan B. Wight (London, 2002), which provides our hero with a thought-provoking second coming.

Turning from biography to interpretation, *The Cambridge Companion to Adam Smith*, edited by Knud Haakonssen (Cambridge, 2006), provides accessible introductions to all aspects of Smith's thought, including his rhetoric, aesthetics and epistemology, although the essay by István Hont and Michael Ignatieff on needs and justice in *The Wealth of Nations*, as well as other essays on the Scottish economy and Scottish academic culture, in *Wealth and Virtue: the Shaping of Political Economy in the Scottish Enlightenment* (Cambridge, 1983) have yet to be surpassed. Thereafter, recommending works from the raft of secondary literature available becomes somewhat personal and partial. That proviso made, I highly recommend Jerry Evensky's *Adam Smith's Moral Philosophy: A Historical and Contemporary Perspective on Markets, Law, Ethics and Culture* (Cambridge, 2005) to students of economics wanting an accessible yet nuanced and comprehensive survey of *The Theory of Moral Sentiments* and *The Wealth of Nations* that locates Smith relative to more familiar economic gods such as Marx, Mill and the Chicago School. Students of philosophy may be more interested in Charles L. Griswold Jr's *Adam Smith and the Virtues of Enlightenment* (Cambridge, 1999) and Ryan Patrick Hanley's *Adam Smith and the Character of Virtue* (Cambridge, 2009), whose account of the crucial Part vi of *The Theory of Moral Sentiments* I find illuminating. D. D. Raphael's *The Impartial Spectator: Adam Smith's Moral Philosophy* (Oxford, 2007) is harder going, but offers a salutary note of caution to those who might otherwise be inclined to paper over the cracks in Smith's spectator theory.

Although it contains only a few references to Smith, Peter N. Miller's *Defining the Common Good: Empire, Religion and Philosophy in Eighteenth-century Britain* (Cambridge, 1994) provides the context for Smith's thought on religious toleration and empire, aspects that risk getting sidelined in our focus on virtue ethics. Although Chapter Two and Chapter Three of Donald Winch's *Adam Smith's Politics: An Essay in Historiographical Revision* (Cambridge, 1978) are useful, there remains something of a gap when it comes to situating Smith relative to his contemporaries' discussion of Britain's 'mixed constitution'. Maxine Berg's *Luxury and Pleasure in Eighteenth-century Britain* (Oxford, 2005) uses the material culture of Smith's notorious 'trinkets of frivolous utility' to link familiar accounts of Georgian manufacturing and industrialization with a less familiar yet persuasive account of an emerging consumer culture built on 'populuxe' goods.

For the relationship between the thought of Smith and Hume, as well as Smith and Rousseau, see Haakonssen's *The Science of a Legislator: The Natural Jurisprudence of David Hume and Adam Smith* (Cambridge, 1981) and Dennis C. Rasmussen's *The Problems of Commercial Society: Adam Smith's Response to Rousseau* (Philadelphia, PA, 2008). For Smith's antique sparring partners, see Gloria Vivenza, *Adam Smith and the Classics: The Classical Heritage in Adam Smith's Thought* (Oxford, 2001).

Acknowledgements

I first engaged closely with Smith's ideas as a doctoral student at
Cambridge, largely thanks to discussions with my friend Ulrich Adam,
to whom I owe a considerable intellectual debt. This book, however,
had its origins in a proposed brief introduction to Adam Smith's works
aimed at history undergraduates, an idea I developed with the help
of a student, Peter Brealey. While adapting it into biographical form
necessitated a complete rewrite, the end product inevitably drew on our
earlier discussions, and I thank Peter warmly. Among the other University
of Southampton students who joined me for HIST3142 and HIST3146 (better
known as 'Passions and Profits'), my year-long tour of Adam Smith's world,
I would like to thank Chingun Anderson, Tim Goodhew, Paul Hipwell,
Paulina Jacubek, George Legg, Scott McCaw, Curtis McGlinchey, Doug
Mackie, Leo Shipp and Alice Trickey. Their engagement made our seminars
the most rewarding experiences I have had so far in my teaching career.

Teaching Smith at a French business school provided a different, yet
equally memorable, set of experiences. Although the seminars I led over
several years of teaching on the Economic Theory and Globalization course
at the École Supérieure des Sciences Commerciales d'Angers were more
compressed and less historical in approach, I thank Thomas Hoerber at
ESSCA for the opportunity to teach Smith in both Angers and Paris. Finally
I thank Ben Hayes for inviting me to contribute to the Critical Lives series,
and for gamely agreeing to let me do Smith when what he really wanted
was a book on Darwin.

Photo Acknowledgements

The author and the publishers wish to express their thanks to the below sources of illustrative material and/or premission to reproduce it.

© Trustees of the British Museum, London: pp. 22, 29, 34, 39, 52, 59, 67, 70, 70, 76, 84, 95, 98, 102, 105, 108, 130, 138, 164; Los Angeles County Museum of Art, www.lacma.org: p. 14; Metropolitan Museum, New York: pp. 10, 18, 26, 74, 111, 115, 147, 157, 170, 173, 175; National Library of Scotland, Edinburgh: p. 46; National Portrait Gallery, London: p. 36; Royal Bank of Scotland Archives: p. 129.